Don't DIE At Wal-Mart!

Harkon Ajala

Don't DIE At Wal-Mart!

The 7 Secret "DON'Ts" <u>Any</u> Average Joe Can Use

That Will GUARANTEE You Retire Wealthy...

...Even If You're Starting Late & From *ZERO* Right Now!

Harkon Ajala

Luxe Life OmniMedia

Indianapolis   **New York**

3

This publication is designed to provide competent and reliable information regarding the subject matter covered. However, it is sold with the understanding that the author and publisher are not engaged in rendering legal, financial or other professional advice. Laws and practices often vary from state to state and if legal or other expert assistance is required, the services of a professional should be sought. The author and publisher specifically disclaim any liability that is incurred from the use or application of the contents of this book.

Published By Luxe Life OmniMedia in association with Luxe Life Dynasty LLC

The "Don't DIE"™ Series is a trademark of Luxe Life Dynasty LLC

Luxe Life OmniMedia

13148 Turquoise Cir, Suite 7

Carmel, IN 46033

Visit our website for a FREE GIFT at www.DontDieAtWalMart.com

Printed in The United States Of America

First Edition: April 2010

ISBN: 978-0-9845005-0-5

The Controversial Content

- for my children, Camara, Nyhle, and Djimon....

Always know daddy loves you with all his heart. I leave this for you so you will never know the bondage of financial slavery.

For my loving, supportive wife and true soul mate Lisa; thank you for your steadfast, unconditional belief in me, and for forcing me to finish this. I love you.

For my beloved father, the late Jerry L. Wilson; a great genius of a man who never got the opportunity to fully actualize his enormous potential... We did it dad. I finished what you started.

For my beloved mother, the late Gwendolyn Wilson; You were right mom. You programmed me for success from birth. You were right.

For my ever supportive baby sis, Siwatu; your understanding meant more than you can ever know... I love you all.

... And especially for every suffering, determined, hard working person, whether 15, 25, 45, or 55 years of age; who deserves to live a life and retirement filled with the joy of freedom from money worries, and has a white hot, burning desire to do so... mad props from a kindred spirit.
I feel you.

Here's a ladder--

<u>Welcome To The Terrordome:</u>

The Most Brutal, Confrontational, Controversial Introduction To A Money Book You've Ever Read.

I want to be crystal clear and frank with you right now friend: if you are a slave to the preachings of traditional personal finance gurus and advisors, if you're a sheep content to follow their advice mindlessly and in blind faith hoping for the best, DO NOT READ THIS BOOK. Close it right now and return it to where you got it. Good luck. I'll pray for you.

Now, if you're still here, I need you to understand the words you are now reading were written as a warning. A blinking, screaming, siren designed to force you to come to terms with one unavoidable fact: *If you keep doing what you are doing right now with your finances you are headed for a fate worse than both death, and eternity roasting in the fires of Hell combined.*

Put simply -- you will spend your retirement and the final years of your life as an old, poor, broken down, ailing Wal-Mart greeter with sore feet; being pitied and laughed at by teenage customers, and bossed around by a 19 year old "3rd Assistant Crew Leader" with his pants hanging off his ass.

Now please... spare me the righteous indignation act and the platitudes about *"who the hell I think I am"* for having the nerve to tell you how your life will unfold.

Denial and acting offended to protect your ego doesn't change the facts. The mountain of economic statistics and studies released every year in the midst of this brutal recession make the facts crystal clear. So do the nonstop foreclosure, bankruptcy, and job "layoff" horror stories we all hear every day, often from people we know personally.

It's simple: if you stay the course you're on, the ugly picture I just painted *is* your future.

But you know what? **It's not your fault.**

See, the road map to The American Dream you've been given is built on a pack of lies that no longer apply in today's world. As a matter of fact, everything you've been told about how to handle your money is not only a lie, but it is the exact opposite of what you need to do to guarantee yourself a life free from financial worries and, especially, a happy retirement. Ain't that a bitch?

Chances are all of your life you've been purposely taught to think and act the way you do with your money the same as I was, because it allows the rich and powerful -- *who already know the secrets I'm about to reveal to you in this book* -- to prosper much easier and much faster.

While you're fighting and screaming over their intentional diversions; *(I've always chuckled at people whining and bitching about taxes killing them when they can't even control their own monthly spending)* in a traffic jam on the road to stress and struggle along with the rest of the crowd, those "in the know" are speeding down an open highway to financial freedom and wealth without a care in the world. All because of the memos you never got.

As this book goes to press, every day I'm watching people around the world in a state of panic as they watch the economy, Wall Street, major corporations, storied financial institutions, and their stock market investments -- *set up as retirement "nest eggs" and guided by their trusty "financial advisors"*-- come crashing down around them.

You probably know very well how it feels.

All the normally "solid bets" seemingly going down in flames all at once, while the cost of gas, food, and everything else is skyrocketing, our paychecks are decreasing, and every Friday when we leave work we hope we have a job to come back to on Monday.

And this is all *after* the U.S. Government has spent almost **A TRILLION DOLLARS** bailing out everybody from AIG, the auto companies, and the big banks, to the CEOs who presided over the whole mess.

One thing you have to give 'em is; those CEOs, women included, have balls the size of Peyton Manning's head.

These brazen, remorseless assholes begged for and accepted billions of dollars in bailouts without an ounce of shame, and then promptly went on weekend spa retreats, presumably to recuperate from a horrendous case of Post-Traumatic Stress Disorder brought on by running billion dollar corporations into the ground and receiving no consequences for it.

Where I grew up that's called pure, unadulterated *pimpin'* of the highest magnitude, awardable with an iced out chalice, a lime green suit with matching derby, and top recognition at the annual Player's Ball.

Yep, the government bailed out everybody but me and you; the actual taxpayers, many of whom, in a stroke of irony almost too bitter to stomach, are funding the cool trillion in corporate welfare with our tax payments while simultaneously looking for a new place to live, having had our homes repossessed by the same banks we are now being forced to "rescue."

Ouch.

But think about this: none of the politicians or financial pundits or "experts" on TV ever mentioned all this could happen when they were telling you it was smart to go ahead and buy that oversized new house, that brand new, gas guzzling, mammoth SUV, Christmas gifts on credit cards for everybody in your iPhone, and all other manners of wild spending of money you hadn't made yet, did they?

Remember the incomparable 'Dubya' telling us all on national TV *(with a straight face)* to "…go shopping, take your family on vacation. Spending is good for the country…?"

Consumerism as patriotism. Unbelievable.

They really fucked us didn't they?

They lied to us and misled us. And the part that really makes you wanna puke is that they did it *(and still do it)* mainly because they so often directly benefit when <u>we</u> commit financial suicide.

But here's the good news: **With this book, there is hope.**

Now if you continue to make the same "broke-ass mindset" financial decisions after you've read it then you cannot blame the government, the greedy rich, or anyone else when you're a 68 year old Wal-Mart new-hire. It will be your own damn fault. As Ricky Roma would say, "Live with it."

The secrets of the mindset taught in this book however, can steer you off the road to ruin and put you on the path to easy street for good, but frankly, you're gonna have to pull your head out of your ass and be open to thinking and doing some things differently. The kool-aid you've been drinking has gotten you in the situation you're in right now.

Time for another flavor.

Speaking of kool-aid, let's get another thing out of the way. Regardless of the "overnight success" fantasy Hollywood is constantly selling you and the convincing promises of the Powerball Lottery commercials, I need you to understand; you probably are *not* going to be Jay-Z.

Face it; like it or not, most of us are not going to be young, famous, multi-millionaires summering in a huge mansion in the Hamptons, driving drop top Bentleys, and posing for paparazzi on the red carpet. Just so we're clear: this book will *not* help you accomplish that. I suggest learning how to rap, how to put up 20 points and 13 rebounds on LeBron James in the playoffs, or how to marry an 87 year old billionaire with severe heart problems and erectile dysfunction.

That being said, what might surprise you is when I asked hundreds of people the question directly, I found that most of us don't really *want* to be one of the filthy rich. What we want is a comfortable, secure life during our working days, followed by an enjoyable, worry-free retirement spent doing the things we love, which for most of us, does not include a minimum wage job.

But I also found we're all very tired of the so-called "experts" telling us over and over to cut back on spending, save money, and invest for our retirement, without telling us *HOW*. That's kind of like telling someone who's 200 lbs. overweight to "just eat less and exercise."

We need specifics. We want clear directions and simple steps that we can actually *do*.

      * *How* do we find the money to save and invest when we're barely paying the bills month to month right now?

      * *How* do we develop the discipline to "cut back," spend less, and save more?

      * *How* and *where* exactly do we invest to guarantee a well funded retirement and still actually enjoy life a little bit today?

I wrote this book to answer these tough questions for real, everyday people; for *"Joe & Jill Six-pack,"* because I didn't see anybody else doing it truthfully and without wrapping it in a bunch of over complicated, self-serving bullshit.

But... it's time for me to be crystal clear and frank again; *this is not a book written to impress intellectual egg heads who want to debate endlessly over stock market theory, political and socioeconomic factors, statistical minutiae, grammatical perfection, and anal retentive documentation referencing the theoretical masturbations of other egg heads.*

I don't have time for all that crap and neither do you.

I'm trying to help people save themselves from financial DEATH, not get presented with an honorary economics degree.

You have common sense.

If you're like most people, you don't feel real secure about the security of your job or the shape of your finances right now, and you don't see many reasons to believe things will get much better on their own in the future. You don't need me to bury you in a mountain of data and footnotes to prove that your money ain't right, and if you do, look elsewhere because I have no interest in trying to sell or convince people.

You either get it or you don't.

I'm not asking you or anyone else to believe anything I say, do anything I advise, or even listen to me for that matter. I'm not saying my way is "the right way" or the only way.

All I know is less than 4 years ago I started off with the same problems, if not worse, that many average, everyday people are struggling with right now in this quicksand mess of an economy we find ourselves in.

I was newly divorced, had just filed chapter 7 bankruptcy, lost my house in the divorce and my rental homes to foreclosure, was sleeping on a friend's couch, and with 3 kids to help support, didn't have a bent penny to my name in the bank.

I was desperate. I had to do something different.

By changing course, rebooting my thinking, and following some ridiculously easy principles and strategies that were very different from what everybody else was doing, I was able to completely reverse my bleak financial reality, so that today while everyone else is terrified because they're not only broke now, but will be even more broke when they retire, I'm totally relaxed. I don't feel a single pang of worry over money in the present or the future.

You can decide for yourself whether or not how I did it, and how you can do the same, is worth an hour or so of your time to read.

If you do have the inclination and courage to read on, don't let yourself get sidetracked by my unorthodox style of narrative in this book, one that may seem to constantly vacillate between seeming abrasiveness and near sentimentality.

Chalk that up to the ongoing, epic battle of the duality of my own nature; which is on the one side a born crusader with an enlightened drive to uplift humanity, foster consensus, and champion the underdog, *(nothing ignites a fire in me more than seeing a bully terrorizing the less powerful)* and on the other, a sometimes aloof, slightly cocky, confrontational and often impatient, smart-ass, with a devilish need to rebel against authority and convention… *and to shake people up a little.*

The same duality explains why I'm a fierce advocate of both social responsibility and personal accountability simultaneously. My friend Damon gleefully calls me a "bleeding heart capitalist." So needless to say, for the next 100 pages or so, I recommend you set aside your own preconceived ideas and beliefs about money, soak up some new ones you're going to be confronted with, expect the unexpected, and just enjoy the ride.

Again, this short, simple book is written for the *average person*, maybe much like yourself, who is working hard as hell everyday and juggling a hundred different things at once just to stay afloat.

You don't have the time or energy to spend learning a bunch of complicated investment formulas or sitting for hours on end at expensive *(and dull as f@#%k)* retirement seminars and trainings.

You don't have $15,000 to $20,000 just lying around in a bank account waiting for the perfect real estate investments to come along, and your credit might not be good enough to borrow money to invest with anyway.

You're sick of trying to read through the latest 640 page personal finance bestseller that's thicker than The Bible and is only number one in a series of 18, written by the same "money expert" who appears on The Today Show once a month hawking her newest release; *and saying the exact same shit she said last month* to sell her previous "must have" book.

Unlike many of the talking heads preaching financial and investment advice to you on CNN, the internet, and talk radio, you probably *do not* become sexually aroused over discussions about "puts," options, interest rates, ROI, bear markets, bull markets, and the value of the dollar against the euro, etc., etc...

Most likely, all that stuff sounds like a foreign language to you *(and a very boring one at that)* and you'd rather be barbecuing

15

or actually having sex.

And I feel you, because that's exactly how I felt.

Just cut to the chase. Cue the short version.

Give me the step by step plan I need to get this money shit fixed in as little time as possible so I can get back to the stuff *people with a life* actually find enjoyable: having fun!

Well here it is. Mission accomplished.

I do have to admit though, *(much to the dismay of my wife's grandmother, Mrs. Ida Martin – told you I'd finish it grandma!)* it took me a lot longer to write this little masterpiece than I expected, because once I sat down and started writing, I became obsessed with getting it perfect for you.

As a recovering perfectionist, I wanted it to be the 'be all, end all' of guides on how the average person can retire wealthy with ease. I wanted you to never have to worry about learning another thing about financial intelligence after reading it. I wanted it to be the only money and retirement guidebook you'd ever need.

Of course, as is often the case when my sizable ego combines with my tendency to pursue audaciously ambitious goals, the final result didn't quite hit the mark I was aiming for.

This book is <u>not</u> the 'be all, end all.'

The great, devastatingly handsome prophet was not able to descend triumphantly from the mountaintop with the only financial holy tablets you'll ever need, *because there's no such thing*, but I can still back my <u>guarantee</u> that you'll enjoy a wealthy, comfortable, secure retirement if you follow this book's simple steps, because while I didn't succeed in including

16

everything you'll ever need to know about personal financial intelligence in this puppy, it *is* the ultimate **cheat sheet.** It <u>will</u> get you there fastest and easiest.

It gives you all the basics you'll ever need, and if your desire to avoid spending your days bagging groceries during your retirement is strong enough to get you to read all the way through it, you'll know what additional learning you may gradually want to undertake afterwards…

…And even more importantly; what extra bullshit to avoid.

See, in the end I realized the best way to make this little book most helpful to you was to make absolutely sure it met one simple criteria:

This is the *exact* book I would have wanted to read when I was exactly where you probably are right now.

Because even before the divorce and the bankruptcy and the foreclosure, I was struggling every month to make ends meet, never seeming to be able to get ahead. It seemed no matter what I did there was always too much month left at the end of the money, and what was most frustrating was; I had no idea why, or what to do about it.

All the conflicting "advice" being shot at me from every direction just left me more confused.

It was a seemingly chance meeting with a stranger, *(I've since come to understand there are no coincidences)* right after the bank sent the Sheriff down to take from me the house my deceased parents left my sister and I; that changed my life forever. This extremely wealthy person, who is a virtual recluse, and who had nothing to gain personally

17

except the joy of helping someone else; was gracious enough to become my mentor and teach me the secret keys to what I call *"lazy, automatic wealth"* that I've now distilled down into **"The 7 Secret DON'Ts"** I'm about to share with you.

Because I followed these same simple but normally hidden principles faithfully, my money problems are now a thing of the past and whenever I decide to stop working, whether it's in my own business or in some job I can't resist taking in the future *(I wouldn't hold your breath on that one though)*, I'm guaranteed to "retire" a multi-millionaire. Today I truly live the life I used to dream about.

But believe it or not, life still isn't completely all peaches and cream for me, because I hate having to watch others suffer unnecessarily.

It absolutely kills me inside to see people, many of whom I love and care about, living miserably because of money problems and knowing that, if they stay on their current path, what's waiting for them in retirement is even worse than the miserable hell of their working days right now.

So this book is my way to give back.

It's my way to serve and help millions of people directly instead of thousands, something I would never be able to do in my live trainings or one-on-one consultations even if I took every day of the rest of my life to do them.

So here's the deal; over the next few minutes I'm going to tell you several, strange stories unlike any you've ever heard, and we're going to have an intimate, one-on-one conversation about them and what their sometimes disturbing messages mean to your current financial life and prospects for retirement, as if I was sitting right there in front of you.

No sugar coating. No holding back. No spin.

Uncut and uncensored.

There's _no_ complex, difficult, hard to follow investment jargon, _no_ arcane, tedious philosophy, _no_ time consuming, complex strategies, and _no_ bullshit filler here.

In these pages you now hold in your hands is that specific, simple, step by step plan that will guarantee you don't end up in the retirement nightmare I described. The same nightmare that, along with most people, you're probably sleepwalking towards right now like an entranced mosquito being hypnotically drawn towards a bug zapper.

It's all laid out here in plain English, and it all takes just a few minutes per month to be put into action. All you have to do is follow it.

This is not theory. This stuff works. I'm one of many living examples. You'll personally see the proof in the pudding for yourself when you see the money starting to pile up and feel the sense of control, security, and POWER beginning to course through your veins _within just 40 days_ of working these secrets into your life.

And let me say in advance; if, because of my burning passion, at times our conversation sounds or feels like _tough love_, just know it is still being offered in nothing _but_ love, and from my passion to serve others.

If that's not good enough then to hell with you. Go back to watching American Idol.

I'm sure they'll reward your faithful viewing and multiple 99 cents votes with generous contributions to your retirement plan. Right?

Harkon Malik Ajala, January 2010 - *from the lap of a beautiful woman somewhere in the Cayman Islands*

Surreal Prologue:

The Horrific Encounter That Forced Me To Write This Smart-Ass Book (And Why You Should Care)

"Let me get the door for you sir, and how are you today?"

A look of horror froze on my face and my mouth hung open for what seemed like a full minute as I searched for words to respond with. The lady who was holding the door for me at McDonald's was at least 90 years old and looked like if some hyper kid accidentally ran into her while racing towards his next sugar loaded happy meal she would break into 42 pieces *(insert Robert DeNiro as 'Max Caty' in "Cape Fear" impression here).*

Her wrinkled McDonald's uniform was greasy, and her worn hat soaked with perspiration from hard work. I collected myself enough to muster up a weak smile, and finally got words to come out of my mouth.

21

What I said: *"Thank you ma'am, but no, let me get the door for* <u>*you*</u>*!"*

What I wanted to say: *"Thank you ma'am, but what the fuck are you doing still having to work!? Not to mention having to work hard pushin' a mop and wiping tables at a fast food joint? You're older than John McCain!"*

Now that second response might upset you a bit if you're one of the more faint of heart, but what *should* upset you is that this elderly woman, with her wealth of wisdom and life experience, and who probably gave some company 45+ years of hard labor, still has to do grueling, undignified work in her 90s.

What should really piss you off is that the poor lady probably spent all of her pre-"retirement" life working hard everyday, and yet still feeling like she barely had enough to pay her bills every month. You should be furious that she almost certainly worried about money constantly and lived in fear, praying no major unexpected expenses would pop up because she had no funds set aside to deal with them.

But what ought to downright offend you *(and scare the hell out of you)* is that there's a 96.8% chance that you are currently living in the same financial position as she was, and are, sadly, headed for the same fate in your "retirement years:" a life of continued financial struggle, crippling stress, and a demeaning job you'll *have* to work until the day you take that final ride to the theme park with the tombstones.

Here's the bottom line short and sweet: If the vision of *yourself* in that McDonald's uniform at age 90 sickens you, then don't let ANYTHING stop you from reading every single word of the rest of this admittedly smart-assed, but 100% pull-no-punches honest, little book.

That's why you should care.

I'm going to show you a way out of the race to nowhere.

The Butt-Ugly Truth

Every morning I park my car in a nearby McDonald's lot and go for an hour long walk along a beautiful section of The Monon Trail in Carmel, IN, a northern suburb of Indianapolis.

It is exhilarating listening to nature as I walk. Breathing in the cool, fresh morning air intoxicates me with a mixture of bliss and gratitude, and I often do my best thinking there away from the cell phones, emails, traffic, and all the other components of the chaotic pace of modern life.

I have to admit that during my walk, because I can remember all too well when I used to be stuck in a cubicle at work fake laughing at my boss's corny ass jokes about last night's Seinfeld rerun, I get a little extra satisfaction knowing that most other people are at work while I'm exercising.

Sounds a little petty and mean spirited doesn't it? Well, back when I was busting my ass to escape the rat race and dutifully following the rules of the 7 secrets I'm about to reveal to you, I was routinely being laughed at, ridiculed, called crazy, and prayed for by many of my friends and family

23

(most of 'em meant well, God bless 'em), so pardon me all over the place if I allow myself a brief, self satisfied smirk every now and then.

My dream of living the very lifestyle I'm enjoying right now strolling along this beautiful trail was what kept me going through that brutal guantlet, and I'm happy to tell you, the payoff is even sweeter than I imagined.

There is no feeling in the world like total freedom. It is phenomenal! Like the joy of being on summer vacation when you were a kid... *only permanently.*

Anyway...

Each morning when I've finished my walk I usually go into the Mickey D's restaurant to use the bathroom, *(I wouldn't eat there to save my life, but that is a whole 'nother book)* and it was during that part of my morning ritual that the fateful meeting with the nonagenarian busgirl occurred.

Here she was barely able to walk, and yet she was clearing platters, wiping tables, and mopping during the ridiculously busy breakfast rush.

Her skin was pale and looked slightly clammy, and her breathing labored as if she would keel over any minute from the sheer physical exertion her job required. It was a truly heartbreaking and sobering sight to behold.

When I told the manager at the front counter she might want to check on the little old lady mopping and cleaning tables because she seemed to be feeling faint, she promptly informed me;

"Oh, that's Granny Conway. She'll be fine. She works hard and yeah, sometimes I worry, but she flat out refuses to take a break or leave early. She says she needs all her hours to be able to pay for her medicines."

"Uh, o-okay." I stuttered, flat out at a loss for words, which anyone who knows me well can tell you, is a near impossibility for me.

I staggered out to my car in a daze and just sat behind the wheel for 22 minutes pondering the grim scene I'd just witnessed.

How in the world could "Granny Conway" have ended up here? After all her years of life, this is what it's come to?

Is this just an isolated oddity or is there something more to it? Are there many other senior citizens slaving their so-called golden years away at minimum wage, teenager jobs?

Imagine my reaction then when, on my way home, I stopped by the local Wal-Mart to pick up some organic grapefruit and as soon as I walked through the entrance I was met by no less than *three* senior citizen greeters!

"Good Morning sir and welcome to Wal-Mart! Would you like a cart today?"

I smiled, said good morning, and tried not to let them see the pity I felt for them, but I don't know how successful I was.

They were working on their feet and apparently would be continuing to do so throughout their entire shifts. The trio of greeters, both of the women and one man, were all clearly well into their 60s or 70s and looked exhausted behind their smiles.

I remembered seeing and reading stories about senior citizens forced to work to pay for their medicine or because they didn't have enough income to *survive* retirement, much less enjoy it, but it hits home a helluva lot more personally when you pause to look into their faces and really take in their plight. As I looked at them, I imagined my own grandmother laboring in their places. Weary and desperate. Defeated. That made it almost unbearable.

I rushed by avoiding the stooped black man's eyes and smiling weakly at the ladies. What if that was my father? I could feel a sickening pain swirling in the pit of my stomach. Sympathy mixed with outrage.

"It's wrong. It's just wrong." I muttered to myself.
"This shouldn't fuckin' happen. Ever."

The Mystery Of "The Rehirees"

When I got home I had breakfast, showered, did my yoga and meditation, and settled down into my comfortable chair in my home office to work a few hours before lunch and maybe catch a movie for my afternoon getaway.

The clock read 10:34 AM, and as I stared at it, the gravity of my morning experience truly began to set in.

Here I was in my mid 30s, retired from a job in the rat race forever, peacefully sitting at home in my bathrobe about to begin the day's work in my own business, on my own time, and under my own direction at damn near 11 o'clock in the morning, while those folks in their 60s, 70, 80s, and even 90s, had been on the clock at Wal-Mart and McDonalds since probably 6:00 AM, working hard on their aching feet for pre-teen wages just like millions of other elderly people in America.

Why such a drastic difference in our lifestyles?

Most of them reached my age before I was even born. Shouldn't they know a helluva lot more than me about most things? Certainly enough to avoid this dead end fate one would think.

But that's the killer. The fact is they *do* know more than me. A whole lot more.

They all have a store of wisdom that can only be gained through life experiences that I simply won't possess until I reach their number of years. Unfortunately, when it comes to the laws of money, their knowledge is almost certainly part of the problem. To paraphrase one of my favorite thinkers, Mr. Mark Twain:

"It's not what we don't know that keeps us from succeeding; it's what we know *that just ain't so* that is our greatest obstacle."

You see, what I "know" about money has led me to early retirement. What most elderly folks "know" about money, including the hard working ones I met that morning, has led them to late *"re-hirement."*

27

So excuse me if I get a little passionate when I see a nation full of proud, senior citizens in such a sad situation.

I get wound up because I feel that after putting in 40 or more years in that prison we all call "the workplace," a person ought to at least be able to enjoy some sweet freedom in the last quarter of their life.

The idea of a comfortable, secure retirement during a person's "golden years" used to be taken as a given in America, but a quick look at the daily stories in the news of downsizing, outsourcing, lay-offs, plant closings, under-funded pensions, pension freezes, mortgage foreclosures, soaring health care costs, and the serious peril that social security and Medicare/Medicaid are in paints a frighteningly clear picture of the reality for all of us today in the 21st century. The bottom line today is:

It is now 100% up to <u>you</u> to choose whether your retirement is spent in pleasure or in poverty.

Your actions alone, starting *right now*, will determine whether you spend your retirement doing everything you always wanted to do, or as a Wal-Mart greeter with sore feet.

Or to put it another way, based on what you choose to do or *NOT* to do, come 65 years old, it's either the golden years or the golden arches for you. The choice is yours.

Now if you've read this far and decided that a gig dropping fries or handing carts to customers from 6am to 2pm at age 74 doesn't sound like too bad a future, then I repeat: I'd strongly recommend you stop reading

28

this book right now and go get your money back.

You're gonna need it.

But if you've decided that white hair and a blue vest isn't a good look for you, then fasten your seatbelt, pull your heart off your sleeve, put a football helmet over your ego, and let's roll.

I'm about to reveal to you the seven secret, little known but extremely powerful things *NOT* to do that are easy, pain free, and will guarantee you a retirement without money worries while still allowing you to live a comfortable, fun life right now!

These are the secrets of the small group of people you see every so often, who are retired, looking and feeling great, and have plenty of money to do whatever they want.

They travel, golf, garden, shop, relax, screw, give to their churches and charities, and spoil their grandkids to their hearts content all day, every day, without a care in the world. If you've ever wondered, *"How the hell do they do that?"* you've finally found the place to get the answer.

However, let me warn you right up front. If you like your truth packaged in a lot of warm and fuzzy B.S. then, again, definitely stop reading right now.

Seriously.

This book is not for you *and I am not the teacher or guide for you.*

I'm going to be blunt, often sarcastic, a little mischievous, display a slightly dark sense of humor, and above all, brutally honest.

But that's because I believe you are a whole lot smarter, tougher, and more sophisticated than a lot of other authors and so-called "experts" give you credit for.

I believe you're the type of person who can handle the truth and

what you really want are the fastest, simplest, bottom line shortcuts that can help you get what you want: a happy life and retirement, both free from worries about money.

If you're like me, it's painfully obvious to you when some "expert" is just telling you a bunch of crap you wanna hear so you'll feel all warm and cuddly and buy more of their books, CDs, and $1,000.00 coaching programs.

Don't look for that here.

100% "B.S. free" is the only way I roll. If you just want to be made to feel good, go get a massage.

These seven, coveted **"DON'Ts"** are presented in a revolutionary manner that, yes, might shake you up a little bit, but they'll get you on the way to a financially worry-free retirement immediately and without requiring a herculean effort on your part.

You'll be able to use them and benefit no matter how much or how little time you have until retirement age, regardless of your income, your credit score, your current financial situation, or whatever.

The only condition is that you be willing to receive them the way I deliver them: Straight with no chaser.

No bullshit. No political correctness.

Remember, I offer the truth; nothing more. *(yeah, that's right. I love Morpheus from The Matrix Trilogy.)*

Still with me?

Ok, then to paraphrase Dave Chappelle: *"Let's get to the good $#%@+!"*

Buckle up.

31

Secret Don't #1:

DON'T Save Money

Now, I know what you're thinking.

You're thinking that some nut has slipped out of a mental institution with the laundry truck, conned his way into Random House or some other book company, and published a tattered notebook full of insane ramblings... and you were the unlucky s.o.b. tricked into paying some money to read it.

Listen to this story however and you'll see why the wealthy and happily retired know this "DON'T" makes perfect sense.

Back in '89 when I was just another broke, horny college kid in North Carolina, I met a beautiful, curvy coed named Sesame during one of my weekend "research trips" to Virginia Beach.

I still remember vividly the Tuesday afternoon that she called and told me the upcoming weekend would be a good time for me to come down and see her, since her roommate was going home to Maryland for the weekend.

32

Now, whatever she actually meant to convey with that invitation, any heterosexual male that ever went to college knows how I interpreted it. You've probably figured out already that even if I had to carjack a church bus at gunpoint, I was going to Virginia Beach that weekend.

I talked one of my boys into lending me his seemingly un-killable Volkswagen Beetle for the weekend, and then turned my attention to figuring the absolute bare minimum of cash it would take to pay for the gas needed to get there and back. I actually recall cursing out loud because gas had just gone up 8 cents to a staggering *89 cents per gallon.*

I calculated how much cash I would need and set about on a quest to beg, borrow, or steal it if necessary, by Friday.

I can still remember figuring that at 22 mpg, I'd need about $21 to get 23 gallons of gas for the 454 miles of driving roundtrip. That I still remember the exact figures 18 years later probably gives you a good idea that the outcome of the trip was memorable, but that's not the point of the story.

You Been Bamboozled Folks

The point is that the $21.00 I spent for 23 gallons represented almost a tank and a half of gas back in 1989. Now imagine that I did what you've probably been taught was smart to do all your life. Imagine if I'd opted to spend that weekend taking a marathon of cold showers and instead "saved" that twenty-one bucks "for my future."

If I'd placed that money in a typical savings or money market account earning an average rate of 3% *(which is a <u>very</u> generous figure to use as an example considering that the rates are actually averaging less than 1% right now)*, eighteen years later guess how much I'd have "saved" for my future?

A life changing $35.75.

That's right. In eighteen friggin' years, I'd have grown my money by only a measly *$14.75*!

But that's not even the worst of it. The real problem is when we consider how much gas that $35.75 would buy today.

With an average price of about $3.99 per gallon in my area -- *courtesy of ridiculously soaring oil prices, supposedly due to the war in Iraq* -- as of this writing, *(It was $2.63 per gallon when I wrote the first draft just one year ago if you need any more reasons to learn the secrets in this book)* the same 23 gallons today would cost $91.77! I'd have actually lost more than 61% of the money's buying power!

It's called *inflation* my friend, and it's one of the reasons why trying to "save" money is a one way ticket to a second career at 'Wally World.'

But even if we put inflation aside, the main reason saving sucks is because the rate of interest paid on savings accounts and other vehicles for saving money is just *way too low*. To fund an enjoyable retirement of your dreams free from money worries, you must permanently accept the idea that you have to <u>INVEST</u>, not save.

The Answer For The Dumb And Lazy

Don't *ever* save money for your retirement. Invest it.

Guess how much my $21 invested and earning just an average of 12% in annual interest in *the right type* of investment vehicle turns into in eighteen years: **$161.49?!**

That may not sound like much, but it buys over 40 gallons of gas today even at $3.99, which is almost double the amount the original $21 would have bought me back in 1989. At the more "normal" $2.63 per gallon from a year ago it would have bought more than 61 gallons, which is nearly triple.

How would you like the money you invest for your retirement now to buy 2 or 3 times more when you retire than it would today? You think that would help you get by without having to stand for six to eight hours per day, sticking little pink tags on useless stuff customers are returning to the local discount superstore?

And you don't need to be terribly smart or to work harder than Kunta Kinte' to do this. This is an answer even for the dumb and lazy, and since I know you're neither, you now officially have no excuse.

Now the big question is: *"Ok Mr. Genius, what is 'the right type' of investment vehicle to get the returns you're talking about?"* Well I'm glad you asked.

Drum roll please because I'm about to reveal to you a little known secret that most financial advisors desperately don't want you to know, and a bunch of 'em don't even know themselves. The investment vehicle I'm talking about is a mutual fund called an *index fund.*

Of course, you may be yelling back right now;

"Aw hell, I've heard about index funds before. This guy's not telling me anything I don't know. What kinda scam crap is this?!"

Well if you already know then you should be well on your way to retirement as a guaranteed millionaire smart ass! If not, there's obviously something else you still need to learn, so pipe down and keep reading.

The key is in how you choose your index fund and the thought process and system you use to fund it. I'll tell you where to get step by step, detailed info on exactly how to do all this for free in just a minute.

First, let's put this example in the context of our goal of a worry-free, well funded retirement.

Since I was the tender age of 18 in 1989, what if I'd been somehow smart enough to not only invest that original $21, but to decide to keep on investing *only* that same amount each month until I was ready to retire at age 65 forty-seven years later. Using the same average of my $21 per month investment earning just 12% annually, I'd happily leave the working world with **$485,788.46**. *Just under a freakin' half a million dollars.*

I know. That doesn't make you rich, but answer this question: would that amount of cheddar help make your golden years actually feel golden? If you don't think so, consider that the annual interest alone on your $485,788.46 nest egg would pay you *$58,294.61 per year*, which is more than the average American earns in a year today while working their asses off 45+ hours every week for a fat, lazy boss with a God Complex.

I Know Your Burning Question

It makes sense to mention at this point the first question I often get from attendees at my Red Carpet Trainings across the country and also from my newsletter subscribers that goes something like this:

"Harkon, I've learned so much about handling and earning more money for my retirement from you that I've been talking to everybody I know about it! But when I told my friend/brother/financial advisor/etc. about your strategy, he/she said there was no way to get a consistent 12% return on my invested money safely using a mutual fund."

"To try to get that type of return would mean I'd have to put my money into some complicated, risky vehicle or venture. Are they right? How can I get the returns you're talking about without risking my future retirement?"

Now I could write an entire additional chapter on who NOT to get financial advice from *(hint: anybody who isn't clearly doing much better than you financially by following their own advice)* but that wouldn't really help you if you're honestly seeking an answer to that question.

Understand, I'm not a certified financial advisor nor would I want to be one so you shouldn't take my word for anything.

All I know is what I was taught by a lazy multi-millionaire, and following his(her?) teachings retired me from the job force in my early 30's and has me on pace to be worth several million by the time I turn 50.

If that sounds like your kind of party then read on, if not, Godspeed and good luck paying 2% to 5% in fees to have your financial future handled by some kid fresh out of college who hasn't been able to use his or her own "expert financial advice" to accumulate two nickels to rub together.

Now, if you'd like to know in simple steps exactly how to use an index fund to get a 12% or higher return on your investments for retirement without having to go to Harvard and get a degree in finance, go to my website at **www.DontDieAtWalMart.com/bookbuyer.html** right now and check out the report under the *"Three Minute University"* section called, what else?: **"How To Get A 12% Or More Return On Your Investments In 3 Minutes!"**

The report is absolutely free and can be read or listened to in about 3 minutes but will be a foundational piece of your retirement solution.

If after you've gone through the report you feel it was helpful to you, I ask that you donate $3 by pressing the "DONATE" button right there on the website. Your donation helps me continue to produce high quality tools, tips, and trainings and be able to give them away for free. If you feel it wasn't worth it, *don't donate.* It's that simple. It's win/win, and it's all good either way.

I trust you, and let's be honest; if you truly feel you've gotten a key piece of the puzzle of retiring wealthy from my report and afterwards you can't give back *3 bucks*, well, you may as well get your application filled out and on file at you know where. That's how "poor" people act.

Whatever you decide, I also highly recommend when you go over to **www.DontDieAtWalMart.com** you sign up to become a free, preferred subscriber to my **"Retire Rich Hot Sheet"** newsletter so you'll get the most current "insider" retirement tips, strategies, free training audios, and videos coming straight to you in your email box, all freshly updated as our economic conditions change. My Hot Sheet subscribers get to take advantage of advance information most of the public won't know until, sadly, it's too late.

I've got a special, **Free Bonus** for you when you sign up for the newsletter that'll make you kick yourself later if you miss out on it, so go get it now.

Can You Smell The Good Life Now?

I hear the wheels in your head starting to spin.

If you're 18 years old or even in your early twenties reading this, you're probably grinning ear to ear and thinking about how you're going to have an off-the-hook retirement by doubling up my example and sticking a measly $42 bucks a month into your investments, then sailing off into the sunset 47 years later with **$971,596.91**. *Just under a cool million.*

On the other hand, if you're a little older, maybe you're thinking;

"My God, why the *@#% didn't somebody tell me all this when I was 18?!!"

"Now what? I've got less than 30 or 20 or even 10 years to catch up and make sure I don't have to work the drive-thru somewhere when I retire!"

"I'm up to my neck in expenses and bills to pay every month and I didn't get this information when I was a kid, I'm getting it later in life so what's the plan for me now? How the hell do I make up the difference in lost time so I can live the good life in retirement too?"

"Wahhh! Wahhh! I want my mommy!"

Relax.

The reality is that most of us *never* find out this information, much less at 18, so this guidebook would be worth less than Paula Abdul's evaluation of talent if it didn't take that into account.

You Must Be %@$#! Kidding Right?

But there's another question that may be eating at you right now, and if it isn't, it should be. It's the 900 pound Gorilla looming over the daily news and endlessly stomping in our consciousness, the proverbial pink elephant in the room of our times. I can hear you:

"You want me to stake my retirement on and stick my money in the stock market? The same stock market that just crashed and wiped out half or more of people's life assets?!! Dude, are you fuckin' crazy?!!!!"

Well, the short answers would be yes, and yes, and... no.

First, understand that no one can look into the future and guarantee what's going to happen in the stock market or anything else, but for the average person, the simplest, easiest way to invest for your retirement is using an index mutual fund, ***if you follow the strategy I'll teach you in the*** *special report over on the website.* There are some other fantastic alternatives like tax lien certificates and, especially, investment real estate, but I'm being realistic; I know that most likely you, like most people with a bunch of daily responsibilities on their plate, don't want to invest the time, effort, and money it takes to learn and master those investment vehicles.

The simple "set it and forget it" quality of my index fund strategy is perfect in that case. It let's you start right away, push a few buttons, then get on with enjoying your life worry free, knowing your future retirement funding is secure.

All that said, the system you're going to learn in this book is a two-legged plan, with a "Plan B" specifically designed as a secondary, backup source of income just in case of any major losses in your index fund account when you're ready to retire. I'm going to cover this for you a little further along when we talk about "Secret DON'T #6."

But also, keep in mind a great degree of the losses many people took during the most recent market crash was *because* they were following the traditional investment advice of their so-called financial advisors and stock brokers, *(you know, diversifying across investment types and classes, targeting "hot" sectors, and all that b.s.)* but even worse, in the special report I'm going to show you why many of them were losing huge chunks of their retirement money because of their "advisors" all along, even before the crash, when they thought the market was doing well.

In the final analysis though, let's keep it real; let's say you use the info in this book and when you turn 65 years old you've got $575,000.00 in your retirement account, and just as you're beginning to use it to fund your blissful golden years of freedom, the market crashes and it loses half of it's value. That leaves you a little over $287,000.00 which, at just 10% interest annually, would pay you almost $30,000 a year. If you've followed the principles of **"The 7 DON'Ts"** in this book you won't have a mortgage, car payment, or any other debts, and you'll have the income from your Plan B I'm going to show you how to set up later on.

So, would you rather retire with at worst, a more than quarter-million dollar, multi-income security net like that, or with the normal less than $20K total the average person retires with today and hope social security is still around?

Based on the elderly I've seen on social security living off of cat food, I know _my_ answer.

Yeah, in case you haven't figured it out by now; *You Need To Go Get That Free Report Now!*

Then come back here with me. In the next chapter, I'm going to share with you how to use the second "Secret DON'T" to help guarantee yourself a wealthy, happy retirement regardless of how little time you have left to invest in.

For now, just make sure you DON'T Save.

Secret Don't #1 *Action Step*

What To Do Right Now:

A. Go **to www.DontDieAtWalMart.com/bookbuyer.html** right now and get the report *"How To Get A 12% Or More Return On Your Investments In 3 Minutes"* under the Three Minute University section, then follow its directions to get your automated retirement investment plan started and/or on the right track immediately.

B. Next, claim your free bonus gift by signing up for my free **Retire Rich Hot Sheet** newsletter. Be sure to check your email daily for my tips to keep you on the fastest, easiest path to investment wealth! They're extremely valuable and they'll make sure you stay two steps ahead of all the crazy changes happening every day in this new, complex world economy we all have to battle with.

Secret Don't #2:

DON'T Pay "The Vig"

"Hey Paulie. Long time no see."

The man speaking was heavyset, 6'2", and a full three inches shorter than the two silent thugs who stood behind him.   He smiled evilly at the trembling man sitting on the bar stool six inches in front of him.

"Uh, hey Vinnie." The trembling man stuttered. *"I - I been lookin' for ya all over. I been wantin' to explain but---"*

"You little lyin' maggot!" Vinnie roared into Paulie's face, which was now completely white and contorted into a mask of pure terror.

The two drunks sitting at the bar next to Paulie grabbed their whiskeys and almost fell down hurrying to a table on the other side of the tiny, hole in the wall dive. Like all the other hard luck losers in the neighborhood who hung out here, they'd come to drown in booze, not blood.

"The hell you been lookin' for me asshole! You know I been where I'm always at! And I don't wanna hear no @$%& explanations, just put my money in my hand so I don't have to get my suit all wrinkled breakin' your frickin' ring fingers!"

"But Vinnie, I just need---"

"But my ass, Paulie!" Vinnie interrupted again. *"I said I don't wanna hear it! Just put twenty-five hundred in my hand or step outside like a man so I can bust your mitts and get on about my evening!"*

Paulie's eyes were now bigger than the kid's Simon Cowell called a "bush baby" on the American Idol tryouts a few seasons ago.

"Twenty-Five!? But Vin, you said I hadda pay back two grand! That's all I agreed to man! It's all I can get!"

"You forgot about 'The Vig' pal. You owe me The Vig for the two weeks gone by since you were supposed to pay me. Every day past the due date I don't have my money costs you."

"Now, I'm gonna give ya 'til next week. If you don't put $2,750 o' clams in my hand next Friday, God help you, you poor, dumb bastard!"

With that, Vinnie snatched the drink Paulie had bought with his last three bucks from the bar counter, drained it, and turned to leave.

45

The two menacing men behind him paused and bared their teeth in smiles that made them look exactly like hyenas licking their lips as their next meal walked unsuspectingly closer.

Paulie watched the hyenas follow Vinnie out the front door, then stared down at the dirty floor. He felt tears welling up in his eyes as he tried to fathom how he could possibly get out of this mess.

He didn't even have the original $1500.00 he'd borrowed and lost gambling on the Mets. How the hell was he going to come up with almost double that in just 7 days?

The future looked bleak. And painful.

The Vig Hurt

If you have ever seen a mob movie, you've probably seen at least one scene like this and know exactly what "The Vig" is all about. If you haven't or don't, well now you know. What you may not be aware of is that most of us are just like Paulie.

Paulie borrowed money for something he wanted immediately and got bit in his ass by "The Vig" for a whole bunch more loot than he borrowed in the first place. To make matters worse, the very thing he originally wanted so badly that he was willing to go into debt for it was quickly gone, so he'd felt even less motivation for repaying it.

Finally, the fact that he was now already late paying the loan back resulted in even more "vig" and more money to repay.

Paulie couldn't wait, and as is always the case for the person who can't wait, he paid dearly for his impatience. His future health was in jeopardy because he *"had to have it"* <u>NOW</u>.

Paulie Ain't The Only Sucker

As I said before, most of us are exactly like Paulie. Only worse.

We put our financial present *and* future in jeopardy and doom ourselves to retiring in poverty because we just have to have everything NOW, and we end up paying "The Vig" big time.

Just in case you haven't figured it out yet, "The Vig" is what's commonly known outside the mob as *interest* and it... is... a... MONSTER! In fact, the awesome power of this monster inspired the saying that all wealthy people know:

"There are two kinds of people in the world; those who pay interest, and those who earn it. Those who pay it end up poor, those who earn it end up rich."

So there's your choice. The truth about interest explained simply enough for a second grader to understand. Just like I like it.

Bottom line: if you don't want to be ringing up high school kids' fast food orders at age 70 while they snicker and hurl insults at you, *you've got to avoid paying interest at <u>every</u> possible opportunity.*

The Even Butt-Uglier Truth

Believe me, I know the practice of not wanting to wait for it, using credit cards or financing to buy it now, and paying bunches of extra money in interest charges forever is what the majority of the public considers The American Way, but friend, that way of life leads to those dirty little words called "consumer debt," as well as some statistics that should scare the living hell out of you.

Studies tell us that:

Currently more than 95% of the public will retire without enough money to live on and will face having to go back to work.

More than 50% are headed for retirement <u>below the poverty level</u>.

Over 39% of the public 55 years of age and older have less than $25,000 saved for their retirement.

More than 25% of Americans would be late on their mortgage or rent if they missed a even a *single paycheck* from their job.

That's 1 in 4 who are 30 days away from foreclosure or eviction from their home. Not good. *(Can you see now why we're in the middle of a foreclosure epidemic?)*

An overwhelming majority of the American public doesn't even have *one month's* worth of living expenses set aside in case of an emergency.

You don't have to tell me, but be honest with yourself: *Do You?*

The picture is undeniably, downright butt-ugly; and that's ugliness you can look forward to for the rest of your life if, like most of the public, *you can't delay gratification until you can pay for everything you buy in cash.*

The Big "Butwhatabout...?" Part 1

Now, before you go into cardiac arrest, *calm down.* I know that most of us will have to pay interest on a mortgage when we buy a home. If you can pull it off, by all means do so, but let's be honest; most of us don't have $175,000.00 or more lying around so we can buy our home outright *(not that this is impossible, just unlikely).*

For the people who are ambitious and want to retire wealthy *and* early, I'll reveal in detail how to buy your home outright in my upcoming book *The 24 Hour Secret* when it's released.

If you haven't already, go over to www.DontDieAtWalMart.com now and sign up to become a free preferred subscriber to my newsletter and I'll let you know when *The 24 Hour Secret* is released. As a subscriber, you'll get a very special offer and discount if you want to purchase it.

Bankie Wuvs U

Know ye this though my friend; when it comes to your home mortgage, please believe your mortgage holder absolutely loves you!

Hell, it's beyond love. The bank you pay your mortgage to is absolutely "Fatal Attraction" level *obsessed* with you.

Haven't you ever wondered why when you buy a home for $150,000 your $1000 monthly payment stretches out for 30 years? I mean, we often sign on the dotted line without a second thought, but 30 years of monthly payments is nothing to sneeze at. That's almost 4 times longer than the average marriage lasts and it's exactly 30.7 times longer than the average celebrity marriage.

You make 360 payments of $1000.00 over 30 years that equal up to $360,000.00, which is $210,000.00 more than the purchase price of your home! All of that $210,000.00 is pure, delicious "vig" *(interest)* and that makes for a swe-e-e-t profit for the bank collecting your mortgage, especially considering that they've held your house as collateral the whole time just in case you didn't pay, which makes it virtually risk free for them if they aren't stupid enough to loan you more than the house is worth. *(Although, for many banks, even that can pay off through the arcane financial magic/counterfeiting they're allowed to engage in called "fractional reserve banking." Google "fractional reserve banking" if you're brave. You won't believe your eyes... or that this shell game is actually legal.)*

The good news is that "The Vig" isn't usually such a killer in the case of your home because of a couple of reasons: First, a good portion of the interest you pay on your house can be tax deductible, which can *sometimes* make the purchase virtually interest free.

Second; your house, if bought correctly, *(for less than it's worth)* is almost surely an ***appreciating*** asset over the long term, meaning it *should* be worth more than you paid for it as time passes.

If your home is worth $500,000.00 when you make your final payment, you can sell it and earn at least $140,000.00 or so more than the total amount you've paid for it. This can actually increase your wealth.

However, let's talk about the real killers of your wealth that you can easily control: the ***depreciating*** assets that you often buy with financing and pay interest or "vig" on over time, which is pretty much everything else but your house.

Death By A Million Paper Cuts

Cars, furniture, TVs, jewelry, clothes, Christmas gifts, vacations, boats, toys for children, toys for adults, and anything you paid for with a credit card, bank loan, etc., are all *depreciating* assets.

The list goes on and on and you're probably thinking about many of these items you've bought and may still be paying interest on right now. This stuff *almost always goes down in value*, not only to anyone who might want to buy them, but to you as well.

It may be hard to imagine how right now, but it's absolutely *critical* to your future retirement that you avoid paying "The Vig" on these items.

Paying interest on this stuff will drain your wealth and kill your financial future one little drop at a time like sand draining from the top of an hourglass. The extra money that you shell out in interest on these purchases amounts to tens of thousands of dollars, and sometimes hundreds of thousands, that you are essentially tossing into the trash can.

These are all dollars that can make your retirement job-free and worry-free if you'll decide *to get paid interest* on them like rich people do. Let me give you an example that will blow your mind. I'm going to start with the first objection I usually get people throwing out everywhere across the world when I train on this.

The Big "Butwhatabout...?" Part 2:
The One That Gets 'Em Rowdy

Let's talk about your beloved car.

"The ride," "the whip," "the wheels," "the hog," "the sled," "the hooptie," or whatever you call it. I've heard the same song over and over:

"But what about my car? There's no way I can avoid paying interest on that. I can't afford to buy a car in cash, they're too expensive. In order to get a nice, reliable car that I like I have to finance it and make payments."

"Wahhh, Wahhh, Wahhh! I want my mommy!"

Let me just be blunt in my answer: ***Bullshit!*** *(I warned you.)*

That is simply a set of beliefs you've been sold, mainly by people and business entities that earn billions of dollars per year because you hold on to, and act on, those beliefs. Let's look at what these beliefs cost you and your retirement plans.

The average price of a new car sold in America today is right at $28,400.00. The average interest rate is currently about 6.94% assuming you have good credit *(and you and I both know that based on most Americans' credit nowadays, that is a BIG assumption).*

That means with a five year/60 month loan your payments would be about $541.78 per month, after only a very moderate down payment of $1000. Some quick addition shows us that $541.78 per month over 60 months plus your down payment equals $33,506.80, which is $5,106.80 more than the $28,400 purchase price. *That averages out to an extra $85.11 per month in interest you've paid over 5 years.*

Not much? No big deal you say? Check this out.

The car you just paid over $33,500.00 for is on average now worth less than $9,000 in *excellent* condition and *if* you can find a buyer. If you want to trade it in to a dealer you'll probably get less than half that.

But that same $85.11 per month you paid in interest would grow to *$7,266.88* over the same 60 months if you'd invested it monthly and were earning just a 12% interest on your investment each year.

Yeah, ouch.

Oh, It Gets Worse...

But here's what should make your stomach hurt...

If after investing the same $85.11 per month for just 60 months, you never put in another dime, and just let the $7,266.88 earn 12% interest annually for 25 more years, you'll have a whopping **$123,537.43** waiting for you!

Would an *extra* $123,000.00 keep you from having to "pick up a few hours a week" at Wally World when you retire?

When you give that $85.11 per month in "Vig" to your friendly neighborhood auto finance company will they do anything to help you enjoy a few of the finer things in life when your working days are over?

Is that new car that you'll stay excited about for a grand total of 22 days after you buy it worth $123,537.43 *plus the purchase price?*

"Yeah, well, what about if I lease?"

Leasing? Please. Don't even get me started. Unless you're doing it for a business vehicle and know specifically how to maximize those tax advantages without ending up in an audit, it's still throwing away your money, especially when compared to the alternative strategy I'm about to share with you. Also, let's not forget that a large percentage of people who lease cars exceed the allowed mileage and have to shell out even more money at the end of the lease term just for the pleasure of turning it in.

At least, if you bought the car with financing you could drive it without a payment for 7 or 8 years after you paid the damn thing off.

"Ok Mr. Know-It-All. So What's My Alternative?"

What's the alternative I recommend? Well, you can buy a very dependable, nicely appointed used car today for $5000 *cash* or less, especially from private sellers who need the money quickly.

Before you start rolling your eyes, here's the strategy: take that same $541.78 you were willing to pay each month for 60 months and stick it into an account *for just 10 months.*

Don't tell me you can't do that. If you do, you're lying.

THIS is exactly what 2nd jobs, overtime, garage sales, and part-time home businesses are for. If you're currently using one of those to help pay the bills... well, you're in serious trouble and I'm really glad you've got this book.

Anyway, now after just 10 months, you've got over $5,400.00 cash to negotiate with and as the sayings go:

1. **"Cash is king."**
2. **"People pay for cash <u>today</u>."**
...and my personal favorite courtesy of Nino Brown/Wesley Snipes:
3. **"Money talks. Bullshit runs a marathon."**

Trust me. I've done it more than once. You can get a very nice, reliable car with many of the extra luxuries you like if you take a little time to look around for someone who needs to sell badly.

Make your purchase contingent on your getting the car checked out at an auto service center. It's well worth any small fee you may have to pay to protect yourself from buying a ride with a major mechanical problem.

Let me tell you this; you may have never experienced it, but it's a beautiful, incredibly free feeling to have a nice car you're proud of without having any car payments you have to make every month! Woohoo! Sweeeet!

Try it. You'll never go back.

Next, now that you've bought your nice, dependable car in just 10 months, take that $85.11 that you would have paid to the finance company in interest each month if you'd financed it, and have it automatically invested on top of your normal contributions for the next 60 months. The resulting extra money for retirement at 12% just 20 years later: *$49,259.76!* You're now thinking and acting the way the wealthy do. You're on your way to the good life.

Ok, But What if...

What if you already have a car payment? Easy. <u>Don't</u> trade the car in early on a new one. Pay it all the way off, then drive it for another 48 to 60 months. During that time, invest the same $85 per month and enjoy the freedom from car payments. Forget the whole *"yeah, but I'll be driving an old car!"* song and dance. Trust me, the idea that someone else really cares what car you're driving is a lie that's been placed in your mind by ads.

I know that's hard to let go of, but once more, you've gotta think in a different way than the masses do if you want your life and retirement to be different from theirs. *Freedom and power is better than material possessions.*

Now again, for the extra ambitious; after you've paid your car off, invest half of what its payment used to be towards your retirement, and save the other half until you have enough to buy *the next car* you want in cash. Either way, life will be sweet!

Now imagine using this strategy with *all* the depreciating assets we usually buy with credit cards or with financing and pay interest on like furniture, jewelry, and clothes. Can you imagine the extra cash put to work *for you* instead of the merchants and banks?

Starting to see how I retired so early?

Get This One Thing And You're On Your Way To Wealth

Write this next sentence down in big, block letters on a clean sheet of paper, sign the bottom of it, and post it up where you can see it every day, then repeat it out loud every time you see something you want to buy:

"Anything Worth Having Is Worth Waiting For."

From now on, whenever you want something, instead of financing it and paying interest so you can have it now, save the money out of each paycheck *first,* and then go purchase it when you've saved enough.

The great epiphany you're going to have very quickly is that there are many things you thought you just had to have that you really don't even want badly enough to spend 30 measly days saving for.

On the other hand, there's going to be a lot of stuff you're going to save for and then decide isn't worth the money once you've actually accumulated enough cash to buy it.

This next sentence is vital to your wealthy, happy retirement so read it a few times if necessary:

If you practice this one, simple "DON'T" you're going to save $50 to $300 or more in monthly interest payments considering that the average household in America is carrying over $11,230.00 in credit card debt alone.

Hell, that means on average, you'll be saving at least $100 per month in interest payments on just the credit card debt. It's reasonable to agree that if we were to combine the interest from credit card payments, auto financing, and other financing that most households are paying we'd have a figure of at least $250 per month. What does that turn into for you if you invest it each month and your investment is earning 12% interest annually? In just 30 years an account with your name on it will hold **$810,877.82** for your spending pleasure!

That's almost a million bucks! Just from investing the amount you're now paying in interest! You don't have to earn an extra dime.

Is that worth postponing a few purchases until you can save up for 'em in cash?

If you don't think so, then I don't know what else to tell you. As I once heard a very wise man who was a good, old country boy say;

"If thet don' light yer fire then yer wood's wet!"

And Now...For The Late Starters

Don't worry, I didn't forget you. I told you I wouldn't.

As much as I wish it wasn't the case, as I said before, the reality is that most people will never get access to this closely guarded knowledge unless they were born into a wealthy family who passed it down to them.

Coming from a very poor family, I was only blessed to discover it because a series of personal tragedies and hardships created a burning desire in me at a young age to become financially free and escape being at the mercy of the money problems I'd seen my parents struggle with all their lives.

That led me to the encounter I told you about with "the lazy millionaire" at the yard sale who would become my mentor and help show me the way.

Still, even many of the people who *are* fortunate enough to be exposed to these little known truths will find them at a much later age when they may feel they don't have enough time to take advantage of their powerful results. Maybe you're thinking right now, *"Yep, that's me. I'm too late."*

If you are feeling that sense of regret and despair just know this; *if you have 10 years or less before you plan to retire you can still keep from retiring into an illustrious second career as a Wal-Mart greeter by using an aggressive, emergency technique I call* **"The $1000 Last Leg Sprint."**

Here's how it works: for however many years you have left before you retire, you are going to implement "Secret DON'T #2" along with the other 6 in this book and...

...do whatever else it takes to invest a minimum of $1000 per month into your retirement fund.

Period. No excuses. No exceptions.

That means if you are starting from absolute ZERO right now, at 12% interest compounded annually, in ten years you'll retire with at least **$235,855.00** to help fund your comfortable retirement. If you want even more comfort when you retire, stretch to at least $1,500 per month and leave the rat race with a cool **$353,782.50** *in just 10 years*.

Now, will that make you rich when you retire? No.

But the interest on that amount alone, even at a conservative 10%, will put just under $23,600 in your pocket every year without touching the original $235,855.00. That's $6,960.00 more than a full time job at Wal-Mart would pay you and it will be a lot easier on your feet.

And let's be honest; if you have 10 years or less left until retirement age and you have less than $200,000.00 already invested and waiting to fund your retirement, you are in serious trouble, and this is probably the best chance you have of retiring with some security.

Now, if you're still busy laughing at my apparent insanity in thinking there is some way you could possibly come up with an extra $1000 per month to invest for the next 10 years, not to mention more than that, well... prepare your feelings for hurtin' again my friend.

I'm going to show you the respect of telling you what you *need* to hear, not what you *want* to hear: If you don't want the ugly alternative of dropping dead from a heart attack at age 68 face first into the Taco Bell burrito you were wrapping, you're gonna have to stop playing the victim and *find a way* to get the money to invest now.

It's time to put your big boy or big girl clothes on, face the truth, and do what has to be done.

Look, by the time you have finished reading this book I will have shown you 7 techniques that, used together, will allow you to unearth a thousand bucks every month to invest pretty easily. If those 7 aren't enough then get a friggin' part-time job for a while for chrissakes.

You'd do it to buy a bunch of crap that you won't even remember why you wanted a year from now or to get your kids Christmas presents, so do it to ensure yourself some comfort and security when you are finally able to stop working your fingers to the bone.

You smile while you're force fed a series of shit sandwiches down your throat at the J.O.B. everyday.

Let's make 'em payoff.

I've already shown you how to find at least $250 bucks per month from money you're already wasting, so you've only got $750 to go.

$750 breaks down to about 23.5 hours per week on a part-time job paying just $8 an hour. You could do that on a Saturday and a couple of nights during the week. If there are two of you, split that in half.

Coupled with this technique, if you're a late starter, *pay close attention to the information I'm going to share with you later in the chapter on "Secret Don't #6."* Taking action on those rather controversial strategies coming up is going to be especially advantageous and critical for you because of your shorter time span 'til "R Day."

Oh, and here's a final tip: if and when you find your determination to start or stick to your **$1000 Last Leg Sprint** plan beginning to waver, stop by and visit the friendly "retired" greeters at your local Wal-Mart and decide if you prefer the alternative.

It's a pretty effective motivator.

Don't Hate The Player, Hate The Game

Ok, I know it's quite possible you may be reading this and saying;

"That all sounds good for retirement but what about <u>now</u>?"

"I don't wanna drive a 7 year old, used car. I want a sick, new 'Three Hunny' today!" **(That's a Chrysler 300c if you are slang challenged.)**

"I don't want to wait and save so I can buy a Coach purse or the newest Prada shoes, I want 'em <u>now</u>!"

"I want that flat screen, 1080p plasma HDTV for football <u>this</u> season."

"I just bought a new house. I'm not going to wait and save to get new furniture to go in it!"

All I can say to you is… fine.

Do you.

Go ahead and buy all that stuff with credit and don't feel the least bit of guilt about it. Enjoy it to the fullest.

Just prepare to be broke and struggling to make ends meet throughout the rest of your working life.

Oh, and you might also want to research which part of the country has the highest paying Wal-Marts so you can move there when you retire 'cause you're going to be broke then too.

As a matter of fact, I hate to tell you this, but you're going to be struggling with money worries for the rest of your days.

Simple and sweet; ***you're going to DIE broke.***

Sorry to be so hard core, but it is what it is. No sense in lying to yourself about it. You don't have to believe me, just don't kill the messenger. Don't hate the player. Hate the game.

This isn't just me pontificating on my opinion. I shared the statistics from national studies with you. As my college psychology professor used to say ad nauseam; *"The proof is in the pudding."*

Still don't believe me? Ok, here's how to test it yourself.

Find someone who's 5 to 10 years away from the traditional retirement age of 65 who uses credit to buy all that stuff and *ask 'em how much cash they have invested and available for their retirement.*

Ask them if, after 30+ years of working, they can withdraw $10,000 in cash from *any source* <u>today</u> if they needed it to save their child's life.

Ask if they'll be millionaires when they retire in a few years…or if they plan on "staying active" when they retire; which in reality for them means working a job because they'll have to. *(Believe me, if you've got enough money, there's plenty of stuff to do to stay active in retirement besides working a $7 per hour job)*

When they give you their answer, and that answer may be just a "deer in headlights" stare, consider whether it validates or refutes what I've said, and then act accordingly.

The Moment Of Truth

So, here's the million dollar question you have to ask yourself friend;

"Am I willing to do today what others don't, in order to have tomorrow what others won't?"

Read that out loud to yourself, then before you answer it close your eyes and visualize in vivid detail the day you retire from your job or career.

How much money is available in your accounts?

As you look at the total amount available to you on your computer screen, are you smiling and giggling thinking about spending the next month on the white sands and crystal blue waters of a Caribbean island, or are you frowning and realizing you're going to have to start looking for "a little part-time job" to help make ends meet?

Are you excited about planning where you're going to live or worried about *how* you're going to live?

Are you enjoying the thought of watching younger people trudge off to work daily while you head out to the golf course or the mall or your garden; or are you dreading the thought of serving people who are 40 years your junior their french fries as they're out enjoying their weekends?

Again the choice is very simple and plain.

If you want to look at the computer screen and happily plan how to spend hundreds of thousands, or even millions of dollars, instead of sadly planning how to earn minimum wage, you've got to be one of the people who *earns* interest, not one who pays it.

Or as our unhappy friend Paulie would probably put it;

"For the love of God, don't pay the freakin' 'Vig'!"

It's too expensive *and* it costs too much.

65

Secret Don't #2 *Action Step*

What To Do Right Now:

A. Make a list of things you want or need to buy including what each cost. Break the cost(s) down into bi-weekly payments you can afford and begin putting deposits in that amount into a *separate* account until you have accumulated enough to pay for the item(s) in cash.

B. Whenever you get tempted to use credit for a purchase, repeat out loud **"Anything Worth Having Is Worth Waiting For."**

C. Visualize your retirement in paradise that you're creating by avoiding "The Vig" *(interest payments)*. Paste pictures that illustrate it *(where you'll live, travel, the car you'll drive, the hobbies you'll have, good times with family and friends, etc.)* from magazines onto a "dream retirement" cork board that you can hang somewhere that forces you to look at it <u>daily</u>. Look at the pics daily and *feel* them as in existence <u>now</u>.

D. Once you pay off your current credit purchases, use the techniques in this chapter to invest the saved "Vig" for your retirement.

E. If you haven't yet, go to **www.DontDieAtWalMart.com** now and get your Free Bonus by signing up for the free newsletter!

Secret Don't #3:

DON'T Graze With The Cows

It's a beautiful spring day and you are walking along a pleasant, tree lined path in a park. You've come here seeking a very special trail: *The Trail to Paradise.*

Those fortunate enough to find their way to Paradise describe it as a wonderful, exciting place where you have the freedom to spend your days doing whatever makes you happy.

It's a place where you can see and experience the most breathtaking, awe inspiring locations on earth. Where you can eat the finest foods, dress in the clothing of your choice, and travel wherever you go in your dream car.

Each night there you drift off into deep slumber as peacefully as a baby and there are no alarm clocks to painfully jangle you out of it. You awaken happily and rested… whenever you're done sleeping.

You know the trail exists because you've listened eagerly many times as those who now live in Paradise spoke of it and its hidden location. You saw the happiness in their eyes and felt joy radiating from their voices, even as they remembered the challenges of finding and following the trail. Clearly; living out the rest of their lives in this idyllic fashion is well worth the sometimes difficult journey they had to endure to get there.

And envisioning yourself living *your* dream life in that magical place has brought you to a monumental and life altering decision: **You've decided to search until you find the trail and follow it to Paradise yourself...** *or die trying.*

As you walk along, your eyes scanning intensely for clues to the trail's location, you come across your best friend just as you're entering a large clearing of lush, green grass.

"Hey what's up? Where you heading?" says your friend, smiling.

"Oh hey! I'm trying to get to Paradise. I heard there was a trail somewhere out in this park from some people who live there and I'm looking for it."

"You're looking for *The Trail to Paradise?"* Your friend replies, their interest obviously piqued.

"Yeah!" Your eyes light up at the prospect of possibly getting some helpful info. *"Do you know where it is?!"*

"Oh yeah." your friend responds. "It's right over the hill. There are a bunch of people heading down it right now."

"Sweet!" you yell as you began jogging towards the hill at the far end of the clearing. Your focus is so intense that you're only vaguely aware of your friend hollering for you to slow down, all the while trying to catch up with you from behind.

As you bound over the top of the hill, your eyes are immediately drawn to a huge crowd of what must be thousands of people gathered around what looks like the beginning of a path carved into the thick wall of a forest towards the west.

"There it is! That's where everyone was going in. Let's go!" your friend points excitedly.

Without a word or a moment's hesitation, you run ahead full speed down towards the buzzing crowd. When you arrive you see that there are two people at the front of the massive mob yelling instructions into a megaphone. From this distance the distortion makes it impossible to understand what they're saying, but they are clearly, very passionate about the message they are delivering to the throng of enraptured listeners.

As you scan the crowd in the area you spot a family member surrounded by several other acquaintances and rush over to them. Smiling, and in a voice loud enough to be heard over the noise, you ask *"Hey! I just got here. Is this the---"*

"Way to Paradise?" they interrupt. "Yeah, the people on the megaphones are giving this group its instructions. Everybody's here! There are so many people they have to give us the directions on how to navigate through the trail in smaller groups before we go."

You feel an electric current of anticipation and excitement crackling throughout the length of your body and can't help grinning involuntarily as you gaze around the area.

"Hey, who are those people over there?" you inquire, pointing at a much smaller group of maybe 40 people sitting at old picnic tables off to the left of the crowd. *"Why aren't they getting instructions to go?"*

"Oh, they've already been." the family member answers. "They've all been taking the trail for many years as have their elders before them. Those people are The Guides. They take turns giving out the instructions and advice passed down to them through countless generations on how to conquer the trail and get to Paradise."

Your forehead wrinkles into a puzzled look as you look more attentively at the small group of "Guides."

They all look rather unhappy.

None of them are smiling and they seem to be paying very little attention to the speech from the podium or the crowd listening intently.

They are very stiffly and dryly speaking to each other with looks that seem almost cynical.

As you move closer you can make out bits of their conversations amongst themselves. You can't believe what you hear. They are complaining!

Every single one of them is lamenting about bad breaks, problems, stress, and what seems to be a general dissatisfaction with life.

"Something is wrong here," you hear yourself thinking. *"This can't be right."*

Your mind reeling, you walk back towards your family member and friend almost in a daze.

"What's wrong?" snaps your friend, reading the look on your face.

"Uh... those people...you say they're the guides? They've been down the trail? I mean, they don't seem very joyous or euphoric like the others I've met. Are you sure they live in Paradise?"

"No, they live in the same place we do."

"They say they've run into incredible obstacles and unfortunate, unforeseen road blocks each time they've traversed the trail so they've never actually reached Paradise, but it's just been because of bad luck."

"They've assured us this is the right trail, that they're giving us the best guidance available, and if we'll just follow it with faith and determination, we'll get there!"

You turn to let this rather unsettling revelation sink in, and at that very instant, see a small cluster of six or seven people you hadn't noticed before entering what looks to be a tiny opening in the denser, steeper forest wall on the far eastern side of the clearing.

"Hey! Who the hell are they? Where the heck are they going?!" you blurt out in rapid fire succession.

"Oh, those nuts?!" your family member and friend answer in nearly perfect unison.

"Those are the idiots who don't believe The Guides!"

One continued explaining with a laugh, "For some reason they think the wisdom that's been passed down from long before they were even born is somehow wrong. Even though everybody else knows the Trail to Paradise is over here where the whole world is going, they say they've watched and studied several people who live in Paradise, and discovered that they seem to be different from most people. So the fools decided to go a different way!"

"To show you how truly crazy they are, you'll notice that they're taking a trail that's in the exact opposite direction of the trail The Guides showed us! The idiots!" They laughed again wildly together.

"That trail they're taking is weird." said your friend, a bit quieter. "Everything about it contradicts what everybody already knows makes good sense. It couldn't possibly lead them anywhere but to misery!"

With this your family member and best friend begin chuckling again with the others and talking more about how crazy the idiots taking the trail to the east are and what a big, embarrassing mistake they're making.

Bunches of people in the group within earshot join in laughing and agreeing with them, and soon it seems everyone is in on the party. You wonder to yourself what to make of it all.

It certainly does seem strange that "The Guides" who are directing everyone to follow their trail *have never actually made it to Paradise,* even with all of the wisdom of the generations passed down to them from their own Guides.

It's hard to understand how *none* of them were able to get there. Maybe the small troop of "nuts" were on to something, but could wisdom that's stood the test of time for so long and been accepted and followed by so many people really be wrong?

What if The Nuts' trail went on for a long ways and turned out to be a dead end? You'd have wasted your time and energy, and have to waste even more coming all the way back. And your friends and family would roast you alive when you returned as a failure. You can hear them now telling you "I told you so" forever. Hell, if only 7 or 8 people out of thousands came up with the idea to take that other trail how good an idea could it really be?

"Yeah, I've probably got better odds of success if I go with what the majority of people over a long period of time have agreed is the best path." you think out loud, the sound of your voice adding to your feeling of surety.

Feeling confident and determined, you fall into the bulging line of people that is now forming from the excited crowd. The megaphone address has ended and the elder Guides at the podium are now encouraging and shepherding the throng towards the beginning of the trail.

As you look out over the mass of people eagerly following each other into the opening in the forest, you can't help noticing how similar you all look to a herd of cows you once saw on a farm, peacefully following one another single file into the doors of a waiting slaughterhouse.

It's Either Shangri-La or
The Slaughterhouse

The point of this story may or may not be obvious to you but let me put it concisely; the reason you've often heard the saying "The grass always looks greener on the other side of the hill" is because it *is* greener!

It's greener because very few cows have the courage to break away from the herd and go over and graze on the other side.

Most cows will live their lives doing what the herd is directed to do by the farmers, and their reward for all their hard work when their milk producing days have come to an end, is a date with a big ass ax blade in the slaughterhouse *(i.e.; for you that means retirement spent as a Wal-Mart greeter, which may be worse)*.

You can probably guess the outcome of following the crowd of "cows" down that trail all the so-called "Guides" were recommending.

That's right. You'd get the exact same outcome all the guides had gotten, and all the guides before them, and so on and so on.

It doesn't matter if everybody in the world says water and dirt makes ice cream, if they all get mud when they mix 'em, you can damn well bet when you try you ain't gonna come up with french vanilla.

Best selling author and multi-millionaire Robert Allen perhaps said it best in his ground-breaking, must have book *"Multiple Streams Of Income"*:

"Watch the crowd to see where it's going, but don't join it."

My father, the late, great Jerry L. Wilson, pounded his own brilliantly simple conveyance of this truth into my head by telling me over and over since my earliest memories:

"Think For Yourself."

The mega-successful business mogul, Earl Nightingale of Nightingale Conant fame put it this way, which along with my father's single, unforgettable sentence, is the way I suggest you commit it to memory;

"... in the absence of any good mentors to follow, just look at what the majority is doing and do the opposite because the majority is always wrong."

You don't need to think very long or deeply to see how true this philosophy really is.

I shared with you earlier that an overwhelming majority of people in America will retire and then die broke. Do you think you need a Ph.D. degree to figure out that we might not want to do what they're doing with their money? As my friend Mike Collins often says, *"that's called a clue folks."*

Let's talk about some of the ways the average, everyday person handles their money:

1. **They buy stuff with credit cards and don't have the money to pay off the full balance at the end of the month.** - The easiest way to guarantee you end up paying a whole lot more money that you didn't have in the first place, for a lot of stuff you can't even remember why you wanted.

2. **They shop and buy things on impulse with no budget, no list, no plan, and without keeping a record of where they spent how much, and on what. Then they wonder where all their money goes.** - I assure you, you're already earning enough extra money to fund your cash rich, Wal-Mart-free retirement, you're just hemorrhaging it out of a million little paper cuts that are unnecessary, impulse purchases. Ever thought about what that $1.69 large coffee you grab on the way to work every day actually cost you?

Well it cost you ***$120,593.75*** if you invested it at 12% interest for the next 30 years!

Unbelievable ain't it? *Imagine how much it's costing you if you're splurging on a #!%@* Starbucks latte' every day!*

3. **They constantly listen to, solicit opinions from, and take advice on their finances from people who are just as broke or "broker" than they are.** - If you want to know how to build a house, ask a builder who's built one, *not* your best friend who hasn't figured out how to build one either, and *definitely not* your uncle who's homeless.

4. **They stress about, worry about, and get more creative than George Bush's Iraq War justification trying to pay everybody they owe each month except themselves, even though they're the ones doing all the damn work for the money.** - Let me say this plain enough for even Paris Hilton to get it: *Pay yourself the first dime of every dollar you earn no matter who else doesn't get paid because of it.* No exceptions! No excuses!

I promise you, any unpaid bills will still be there next month, but nobody you pay instead of yourself will be there to hand you a check when you retire as a reward for your thoughtfulness.

From now on, every time you get your paycheck, say out loud to yourself:

"Why the hell would I be willing to float checks, get payday loans, work overtime, borrow from friends and relatives, use credit cards, setup payment arrangements, borrow from my 401k, and take any other number of desperate measures to pay some company that doesn't give a damn about me, and not be willing to do the same to pay myself for all my hard work?"

Keep repeating this every pay day until you have the same sense of crazed urgency to fund your retirement investments as you do to keep your damned cell phone on.

5. **They obsess over and go into debt buying "status symbols" like luxury brand cars, expensive toys, over priced homes, private schooling for their children, designer clothes, purses, shoes, watches, accessories, etc. in an attempt to** *look* **"successful" to other people.** - I've got bad news for you friend; after all your sacrificing, robbing Peter to pay Paul, working second jobs, credit card maxing out, home equity loans, and everything else you do to buy all this crap to impress people... NOBODY GIVES A DAMN.

There's nothing wrong with having this stuff, but don't spend a penny on any of it until you've paid *yourself*, then all your necessary expenses.

I promise you, no one is sitting at home starry-eyed and raving about your Gucci bag or the 22" rims on your Escalade EXT. If it's not theirs, then neither you nor your bling is going to occupy anyone else's mind for more than a few seconds.

Here's even worse news; all that stuff will be out of style and long gone when you're a 74 year old, McDonald's closer because you spent your whole life and all your cash trying to be admired by other broke people.

6. **They waste hundreds and sometimes thousands of dollars every year on the pipe dreams of gambling and lotteries.** - Look, it's fine to budget some money for entertainment and go gambling at a casino or whatever if you consider that fun, but when you find your self saying stuff like, *"Hmm, I'm short on money this month. Guess I'm gonna have to* *'go to the boat' and win my mortgage,"* you need to immediately seek out a crack rehab facility because you are clearly smoking it.

If you can ever recall spending time with a friend excitedly discussing the "system" you've developed for hitting the Powerball jackpot or the "science" behind winning at the roulette table in the Flamingo, you may want to go ahead and cancel any appearances on Jeopardy you had scheduled because you're not the sharpest knife in the drawer.

If you've ever looked up and found yourself in a Speedway gas station at 9:54 pm on a Friday night, standing in a 15 person long line, nervously watching the clock and wanting to physically harm the elderly lady at the front of the line who's fussin' about "puttin' in her numbers" because you've only got 6 more minutes to get *your* numbers in for tomorrow's Lotto drawing... please drop the scan-tron card that's probably in your hand right now, drive to the nearest mental health institution, and have yourself committed for psychiatric in-patient care.

Do not pass go. Do not collect $200.

No matter how many ladies on your church usher board testify about how God "blessed them" with their light bill money at the slot machines on the riverboat; I assure you gambling, scratch-offs, bingo, and "P-Shake" tickets are not recommended as part of your financial plan.

Donald Trump owns casinos and governments run lotteries for a reason friend: They generate shitloads of money because the house *always* wins, which means, in case you haven't figured out or accepted this yet, **YOU** *always lose.*

Funny thing is, if you're fighting this truth about lotteries and gambling "systems" in your mind right now, or just plain calling me a didactic, *(gotta use those $100k words I learned in college sometimes)* know-it-all, asshole, ironically you may be right about one thing; *these are not games of chance.*

They are carefully devised profit schemes that are guaranteed with mathematical certainty to deliver the winning odds to the casinos or lotteries. Even if you win some money, you will put it all back and more into the casino or lottery over a long enough period of time.

That's why millionaires *build* casinos instead of using their money to buy millions of Powerball Lottery tickets. Again, that's called a clue.

7. They go into tens and sometimes hundreds of thousands of dollars in debt to pay for college education and college courses but won't spend $50 educating themselves with training from people who are successfully "doing it" in the real world, not just teaching theory in the educational one. - This is a big one and yes, it's controversial. A lot of people get real hot under the collar when I go here and I understand why. Many of them have a whole lot of time, money, and sweat already invested in this bill of goods. Still, don't shoot the messenger. The proof is in the pudding.

Look, there's nothing wrong with formal schooling or going to college. It's a good place to get a well rounded education and a great place to have a damn good time, but if you have a college degree *(or you know someone who does)* let me ask you an honest question; has that piece of paper been the golden ticket to the dream life they sold you -- oops I mean *told* you -- it would be?

Was the high paying, secure job with the big mahogany desk and furnished office laid out and waiting for you when you graduated or are you in a cubicle surrounded by file cabinets and printer paper like everybody else?

See, here's the real deal they never taught us while we were going into twenty years of debt to pay for our college educations: In the real world, you don't get paid for book knowledge, or spouting theory, or good grades, or being able to memorize and regurgitate facts *(unless you can get on Jeopardy and win)*. You get paid for quantifiable *results*.

You get paid for the *value* you deliver to whoever's paying you, calculated by the identifiable, measureable results you produce. Period. End of story. Anyone who tells you different is lying to you.

Wanna know the best place to learn how to get whatever results you want *in the real world?* From people already getting those results in the real world. You've got to learn what they did and how they did it and then model their actions and *especially* the way they think.

Oh, they didn't tell you? That's another big difference between "the blackboard world" and the real world; it's okay to copy in the real world. In fact, out here it's wholeheartedly recommended.

More times than I can count I've heard a mentor and business partner in one of my ventures repeat;

**"It's okay to be a copycat, you just have to make sure
you copy the right cats."**

81

Friend, you've got to accept this as hard truth from this point on; *you are 100% solely responsible for getting your own real world education by reading books, observing the world, studying CD or DVD programs, attending trainings, and mentoring with people who are achieving the success you want.*

That especially applies to building wealth and preparing for retirement since, curiously, none of this is actually taught *at any level* of our traditional educational system *(In fact, you'll find most teachers and college professors can't even correctly define "financial intelligence.")*

And yes, you'll have to pay for it, but here's the good news; some of the most valuable books, audio, and DVD training programs by experts I've come across, as well as the ones I've personally authored, are $15 to $60 bucks at the most, with some in depth, intensive courses costing less than $500 in their entirety.

Many of these will give you the educational equivalent of a year of college or more in just a few short hours of reading or listening. Plus you get to "go to class" anytime day or night around your own schedule, in the specific subject you want training in, and taught by someone who has *done* it... and you won't need a student loan bigger than a mortgage to pay for it.

To help get you started, I'm going to give you as part of your free bonus, my much clamored after, exclusive inner circle audio training *"DON'T Pay Your Bills!"* and a private copy of my most treasured list of the books, audios, programs, tricks, and shortcuts that I personally use and give my highest recommendation to when you subscribe to my free **"Retire Rich Hot Sheet"** newsletter at **www.DontDieAtWalmart.com.**

One thing you can feel comfortable about is that every book, program or course by another expert that I recommend to you, I have given the acid test by purchasing, reading and using myself.

I've been extremely picky; and careful to list only the programs that over-deliver, meaning those that are worth at least three times their cost, because I want you to be blown away by their effectiveness and value. This way you can develop the critical habit of the wealthy, which is to constantly invest in your own education and personal development.

If you decide to snatch up one from my website, I may receive a small percentage of the sale as commission for leading you to it. I have no shame or hesitation in telling you that because I know as long as you experience a major benefit from them, you could care less. I recommend these hand picked training tools to you with complete confidence because each one of them has played a part in helping me retire 30 years early and free from worrying about money *(or time cards)*.

So now you know exactly why "the cows" live the subservient life they live and why they end up where they end up when their working days are over, *(when they're "retired" you might say)* because we've examined seven of the most counter-productive things the majority of people *(cows)* do with their money.

Obviously there are bunches of other mistakes the majority makes, but these are probably the ones that most put them on the fast track to fast food employment during their retirement. The only question is; are you going to be there covering their position at the fry station when they take a break?

Whichever is the case, it's up to you. It's your decision.

You decide whether or not to take the road less traveled financially in order to eat the greener grass on a different side of the hill; just know that your decision will ultimately determine whether you spend your retirement in Shangri-La, or in a bloody slaughterhouse.

And know that you are making that decision even right now, as you hold these pages in your hands and decide whether or not to act on the revelations in them. There's not a damn thing I, or anyone else, can do to be able to make it for you.

My advice is... *DON'T graze with the cows.*

Secret Don't #3 *Action Step*

What To Do Right Now:

A. The action for you to take from now on is pretty uncomplicated; **Don't make the 7 critical errors listed in this chapter like most "cows" do.** If you're doing so now, STOP. *Even if you just do the opposite of these fatal money missteps,* you'll be well on your way to lovin' your life today as you work *and* tomorrow when you retire.

B. Remember, if you've decided you don't want to end up retiring broke *like* most people, you have to think and do things differently with your finances *than* most people. Again, in most cases, *you need to do the exact opposite.* Begin implementing the Action Steps of the first three "DON'Ts" you've learned so far, and begin *today*.

Or you can stick with the majority opinion... go with what you've always heard, and get what the majority's always gotten financially; the short end of the stick.

Secret Don't #4:
DON'T Think Big

"I'm tellin' you, I'm going to be the hero!" the small boy screamed at the top of his lungs with delight.

He danced around tossing the ball he'd just gotten for his birthday in the air and catching it.

"I'm going to be a superstar basketball player like 'Bron James! I'm going to hit the winning shot in the NBA finals that makes my team the World Champions! I'll be the MVP and everyone will cheer for me and want my autograph!"

"Ha, ha, I believe you will Davie! I believe you will." The young boy's dad answered smiling.

He couldn't help but chuckle to himself at how cute the kid's mispronunciation of LeBron James' name was, and like any parent would be, he was elated at seeing how happy his child was with the present he'd presented him with for his 7th birthday.

The boy was wholly mesmerized with the ball and it seemed to be bringing his grandest dreams to the surface.

"See dad, watch me make a 3 pointer!" little Davie yelled as he tossed the ball towards the 30 gallon trash can in their garage.

The ball wobbled strangely in the air and landed on the concrete floor a good four feet to the left of the can, but Davie was not discouraged. He ran giggling to retrieve the ball and began hoisting it into the air again.

"I'll be on TV dad giving interviews with that lady with the mic'phone, and wearing my Nik-ee shoes with my name on 'em. See, I'll have my own shoe commercial like the other stars! Then everybody'll wanna play me on the Xbox 360 game 'cause I'll be dunkin' with my 'Air Davie' shoes on!"

The boy grabbed the ball and ran towards his dad. *"I'm ready for the NBA championship dad! Can you take me to get on TV with 'Bron James?"*

Using every bit of self control at his command to keep from laughing too hard and possibly hurting his son's feelings, the father scooped his boy up in his arms and held him in a hug before he answered.

"Well, don't you think you ought to start out a little smaller than the championship game on national TV son? There are a lot of steps on the way to the big stage of the finals."

The little boy's mouth turned down into a disappointed frown.

"Why daddy? With this ball, I'm ready to go on TV now! I wanna be rich and famous and shoot the winning shot! I wanna be in the big parade and say I'm going to Disneyland in the TV camera! What else do I gotta learn to be a basketball superstar? I'm da man!"

The man looked thoughtfully into his young son's eyes. He didn't want to temper his son's spirit so he was extra careful to deliver his next sentence lightly and with love.

"Well... the very first step son would probably be for you to learn what a basketball *is*. That brown, pointy thing I gave you for your birthday, and that you've been shooting at the basket all day, is a football!"

Domination By Inches

Little Davie's story illuminates one of the critical mistakes I see many, many well meaning people making.

At speaking engagements and trainings I often speak with all kinds of people as they come up afterwards to meet me personally, tell me how they've benefited from the session, and sometimes ask me to sign books and CDs. I love listening to their stories and soaking in their energy.

I always ask them about their personal goals and endeavors, and marvel that so many of us are so blindly focused on huge, lofty dreams of fast riches, big houses, sexy cars, and various other expressions of outrageous fame and fortune. Without a doubt, the sellers and marketers of "bling culture" have done a helluva job on our asses.

Now don't take me the wrong way.

It's absolutely essential that you aim for dreams as big as you personally desire and do so without an ounce of shame. Anyone who knows me personally will tell you I sure as hell do.

The problem is most of the people who tell me about the big dreams and goals they have don't seem to have given much thought to the series of incremental steps and sacrifices, and small positive actions that need to be strung together in order to get to those BIG payoffs.

One of the most life changing books I've ever read that perfectly explains this great truth in easy to understand detail is called *The Slight Edge* by Jeff Olson. I still remember the moment I understood and internalized the powerful idea at the core of this short book a few years ago; my life began to get better and better every single day and still does. There's a link to check out this masterpiece in paperback or CD Audiobook on my website at **www.DontDieAtWalMart.com**. I'd highly recommend you get your hands on a copy immediately.

Its great revelation in a nutshell is this:

Nothing is static in our lives, we are always moving in one direction or the other, either up or down, backwards or forwards.

Huge achievements and breakthroughs happen because of the compounded effect of lots of small, positive actions and wise decisions you take consistently over a period of time.

Major losses and regressions happen because of the compounded effect of lots of small, negative actions and errors of judgment you make consistently over a period of time.

Read that paragraph *again*.

One of the most powerful secrets I could ever give you to creating a plentiful retirement for yourself is woven into those few sentences, and so is the key concept of this very little known "DON'T."

Dream BIG. THINK small.

In other words, don't think big. *Dream* big.

But *think small.*

Just remember for a moment the last major money crisis you had. It may have been when you took your car in for a routine oil change and one of those evil magicians we like to call auto mechanics waved their magic wand and transformed it into an unanticipated $3,652.00 estimate for "absolutely critical" engine repairs.

They assure you of course, that if you don't get the repairs done:

"Your engine could lock up out there on the road and it'd have to be completely replaced, which could be five times more expensive. It's serious and urgent. You need to get this fixed NOW!"

"Would you like to put this on your Amex or your Visa?"

Or perhaps it was when someone didn't repay you the money you loaned them when they promised, or your paycheck got delayed over the weekend which left you without enough money to cover checks you'd already written.

A couple of those checks bounce Friday afternoon and *voila'!;* they set off a chain reaction of NSF fees more deadly to your finances than the start of the Christmas season combined with the Disney Channel toy commercial brigade. *(Friggin' diabolical, brainwashing mouse!)*

By Monday your account may be overdrawn by $327.00, which of course means that even when you your paycheck *is* deposited you may not have enough to cover your anticipated expenses after the overdraft charges are deducted, which leads to late fees, and... well, you know the drill.

Ever been there? I have. More times in the past than I like to admit.

Whether it's a $300 problem or a $3,000 problem, it may appear to have been a big, unforeseen misfortune, a major miscalculation on your part, or someone else's devious plotting, but if we think *small*, we can uncover a series of tiny, negative actions or errors in judgment we made along the way that helped put us in position for the financial crisis.

What if you'd been contributing regularly to an **I.C.S. Emergency Fund** over the last 3 years since you had the car? *(I'll explain this abbreviation in "Secret Don't #7." Ha ha! It's called "suspense" baby!)*

Even $50 per month would have given you *$1,800.00* to use towards the repair. Would that help?

You couldn't afford to do that you say? Hmmm. That's a measly $1.66 per day. Could we have gone without one less soda for that benefit?

It would have certainly erased the overdraft problem effortlessly. You would've had plenty of money to cover the unforeseen shortage and avoid the NSF charges all together.

Or how often have we not had money we needed on us because we hadn't taken the time to plan and ending up grabbing $20 out of a foreign ATM? *(I call these "Anal Tax Machines" 'cause when you use 'em, they tax you out of you're a--- well, you get the reference I'm sure)*

91

That's a $2 buck charge from your bank and $2 more charged by the foreign bank. $4 of your hard earned cash down the drain every time you play.

I know for a fact that many people self mutilate their finances this way at least once a week because I used to be one of them. That adds up to a total of *$208.00* figuratively thrown into a bonfire every year or -- if you've got a stomach that can take this info -- assuming a 12% annual return, *you're giving away an extra $56,220.86 from your retirement 30 years later just to access your own money!*

See how thinking small can lead to big gains in your financial health?

How about the $8 you spend for lunch every day? That's $2,112.00 per year or **over six grand** you've pillaged from your comfortable retirement over the last three years you've been doing it.

If you'd just taken your lunch *every other day* the last three years you'd have had the money you needed to fix your engine. If you invested the $8 you saved just *every other day* at 12% for the next 30 years; say hello to an extra **$285,000.00** to spend in your retirement years!

I hope this repetition is beginning to permanently paint a picture in your mind. As it says in a short story I wrote called *"The Magic Sentence;"*

"Money is like water. Catch enough of the little drips and you'll soon have buckets full." – *Harkon Ajala*

There are hundreds of little wise decisions and positive actions you can take with the money *you're already making* that will add up to huge amounts of extra funding for your retirement and even your current lifestyle. Discovering and acting on these will have a gargantuan impact on not only your ability to have a stress-free, enjoyable retirement, but also a fun, abundant lifestyle right now. Imagine the money you'll have free to spend any way you please -- guilt-free -- after you put the necessary amounts into your retirement plan each month.

Remember; the key is not to think big, but to think small, positive actions repeated over and over. The compounding effect of those tiny actions then lead to massive results, like a tiny drip of water from a stream wearing a hole through 3 foot thick canyon rock over time.

Or...

...you could wait until you retire and be *forced* to think small as you cash your minimum wage paychecks from a certain retail superstore.

Secret Don't #4 *Action Step*

What To Do Right Now:

A. For the next 14 days take a notebook wherever you go each day. Go about your normal routine and simply write down EVERY time you spend any money. I don't care if it's a penny. Write down how much you spent, and what you spent it on. Don't try to spend more wisely, just record every single expenditure.

B. Now at the end of that 14 days, go back over your records and circle each time you spent money on something you really didn't *have* to have. Notice any patterns? Now put a check next to enough circled items to bring the total of their added amounts to $25.

Maybe it's the second cup of coffee in the morning. Maybe it's a bag of chips and soda as a daily snack. Maybe it's $4 in ATM fees! Maybe it's the $7 daily breakfast from McDonald's. Whatever they are, just chose $25 worth of unnecessary expenditures and commit to eliminating *just those* for the next 90 days.

C. Next, open a separate savings account with *no* ATM card and for the next 90 days, each time you get your paycheck, have $25 automatically deducted into your new **"Security Account."** If for some reason you just can't get it automatically deducted, then each time you get your paycheck, immediately and before paying anything else, take $25 and deposit it into the account.

After 90 days, find an additional $10 you can eliminate every 14 days until you have $50 per paycheck automatically deducting into your account. Now from the day you open the account 'til one year later, if you ever have *any* bonuses, extra money from overtime, have money given to you as a gift, find money on the ground, trade in some Coke cans, turn tricks, or whatever, make sure you put *50%* of the extra money into this account immediately.

Now here's the most important part:

D. Commit to yourself that you will not touch this money for <u>any reason</u> in the next 12 months. This is money you would have spent or didn't plan on having anyway, so not touching it shouldn't negatively affect your life or finances. You need to let it accumulate and grow. Of course, if you can find more than $50 per paycheck you would have spent unnecessarily to sock into this account, go for it. Put in as much as you can find, but *don't* take money that isn't extra, or that you wouldn't have normally "blown" anyway. This is your reward to yourself for your hours of hard work every day. You are rewarding yourself with security.

Just picture what your life will be like two years from now when you're using this strategy to recapture and redirect $100 per month of what used to be money disappearing without a trace to who knows where.

You've now got a minimum of over <u>$2,200.00</u> in your personal Security Account or I.C.S. Emergency Fund to keep any unforeseen obstacles that pop up from raising your blood pressure.

Imagine writing a check without a second thought for a $1,500 car repair that just 24 months ago would have had you trying to figure out how to produce and sell 50 pints of blood.

$250 more needed than you planned on for your kids school and book fees? *Write a check without a second thought.*

Paycheck a little short from some time you had to take off unexpectedly? *Write a check to cover it without a second thought.*

The beauty of it is that the account will be replenishing and growing automatically so you never have to worry about it!

So now you have another critical **"Secret DON'T"** that will help guarantee your retirement is secure and happy, and a plan on what you *should* do to take advantage of it, all without having to work another second to earn another penny of income than you do right now.

Remember; if you're more ambitious, have less time to work with, or just want to live and retire with a more luxurious lifestyle, I'm going to share with you some extremely powerful *(but also extremely misunderstood)* ways to *generate more money* coming into your household in a chapter coming up very soon, so stay right here.

I guarantee after I reveal them to you, you'll have a pretty clear idea of how I retired so early.

P.S.: I Know, I Know. Somebody's Always Got A Damn "But..."

On the highly unlikely, outside chance that you're shaking your head right now and saying;

"But what about me? What can I do in my situation? I honestly can't find even $25 per paycheck of money I'm wasting that I can redirect into my Security Account. That's how tight my money is!"

Well frankly, I find it hard to believe you're being totally honest with yourself and that you've truly followed the expenses exercise I just went over in order to find the cash you're spending unnecessarily.

Are you telling me you're not blowing an extra *$1.78* per day somewhere you don't have to? Hell, if you've got kids they're probably stealing that much from you every day, but for the sake of our conversation I'll give you the benefit of the doubt and assume you're being truthful.

If so, all I can tell you is you need to *run*, not walk, down to the local Wally World today and pick up a part time job so you *can* put away $25 measly bucks every two weeks. If you don't now, you're gonna be on staff there when you retire anyway if your current money management habits won't let you scrounge up even that paltry sum.

Go get the damn job now and get it over with.

You *really* can't afford to think big.

Secret Don't #5:

DON'T Make Long Term Decisions For Short Term Thrills

"Mr. and Mrs. Brokeminesett; I'm here to inform you that your home has been foreclosed on by The National Bank of Vig, and that it is my duty to remove you and all of your belongings, and take possession of this property immediately."

You vaguely notice the Sheriff and the two deputies with him avoiding your eyes out of pity but you're too stunned to feel anything but numb. You want to say something, but you can't even begin the process of forming a coherent thought. You're consciously having to tell yourself to breathe now.

As the gravity of the Sherriff's words begin to sink in with full force, there is a single sentence playing over and over in your mind;

"This can't really be happening. This <u>can't</u> be real."

The deputies move past you to begin removing your life's belongings from what used to be your home and a memory is triggered. You close your eyes and vividly see a reenactment of your family's excitement the day you moved into this house just like you're sitting in a darkened theater watching a movie.

Your mouth goes bone dry.

You feel a lump growing in your throat.

You're ripped from your mind's theater when you become aware of your spouse and children standing behind you crying quietly and staring helplessly at the uniformed men, who are dispassionately entering what was until minutes ago, sacred ground; *your private home.* Your sanctuary.

Dread fills you from painful humiliation. It's dinner time, early evening, and all of your neighbors are watching from their windows and doorsteps as everything you own is set out on the sidewalk in front of your family's former residence. You're moving towards becoming physically sick as you feel your children's fear and bewilderment.

How will their schooling be affected? How will your spouse be able to bear the embarrassment at work or in church? How will you ever again look them in the eyes?

Never in a million years did you ever imagine being in this situation. Your mind still fights against accepting it as reality and not a

99

terrible nightmare that you'll soon wake up from screaming and sweating, but glad it was just a dream. But the cold, business like voices of the men deconstructing your life inside your home -- *well, inside the bank's home* -- mark this nightmare as all too real.

How did it get to this point? It seemed at one time not long ago that you had enough household income to pay for everything fairly comfortably. How and where did your finances get so drastically screwed up? And what the hell do you do now? You've still got bills you can barely afford to pay and have no idea where the money's going to come from to even *begin* rebuilding from this.

Your worst fear has come true before your eyes and all you can do is stand by watching cluelessly with your mouth hanging open like;

"Wha' happened?"

When you bought your home you knew the mortgage was $200 more expensive than the apartment your family had been living in but, based on your calculations, you and your spouse were earning enough money to handle it and felt the increase was worth the privilege of home ownership.

How'd you manage to get three whole months behind on your mortgage? Were there that many new or unexpected expenses to put you in a hole so deep? True, you bought a few things, but they were all necessities weren't they?

The $128 monthly jump in the heating bill during the winter months caught you a little off guard and sure as hell wasn't a pleasant surprise, but what could you do about it? It was a necessity and, again, part of being a homeowner.

Of course, when you moved into your new house you had to make sure it was furnished properly didn't you?

You had to get the appropriate furniture and a big screen, LCD, High Definition TV for the new family room didn't you? Your old living room television set just didn't really match the feel of the newly built home you purchased and the finished basement you wanted meant more space to furnish.

With larger bedrooms the kids each needed their own dressers and curtains, comforters, and accessories to complete the décor. Plus, you needed new furnishings for your master bedroom and bathroom with the jet tub and separate shower you'd always dreamed of. Why buy the house if you're not going to make it into the warm, comfortable home your family wanted?

Naturally you bought rugs and curtain rods and the various other odds and ends people buy when they move to a new home but hell, isn't that what you're working so hard everyday for?   Besides, you were able to get all the new furniture, TVs, accessories, and what not, through the department store's in-house financing plan so you were able to pay for it all in a combined monthly payment of just $179 for 36 months; *and you didn't even have to make your first payment for an entire year.*

You were able to fill the beautiful kitchen in your home with brand new, state of the art appliances through what you felt was a damn good deal from your home builder. They were able to get the cost of the stainless steel, matching side by side fridge, top quality range, dishwasher, built in microwave, a gleaming, electronic range hood, and even a trash compactor, all built into your home mortgage. Spread out across the 30 year term it only cost an extra $42 per month on your monthly house payment! Was that not smart?

Your new home had the deck you always wanted in back so you needed a barbecue grill and outdoor furniture, plus you had to get a good lawnmower and other tools for the upkeep of the lawn and landscaping; but hey, you got all this at no payments for 6 months on your Lowe's card and when the payments started after a half year they were just $47 per month.

Once you moved in you took advantage of a great deal on an alarm system to protect your home and family's safety. This only made sense as far as you were concerned. ADT put in the entire system and waived the $149 installation fee plus gave you the equipment free. All you had to pay was the $38 monthly fee for the system and monitoring.

So what did you do so wrong? What did you buy that could really be considered anything but a necessity? You don't see where you were splurging on anything extravagant like an idiot. You basically seemed to be living like the average American family; like everyone else in your subdivision.

A year after moving in, you and your spouse thought it would be a good idea to get an SUV like you saw so many other people in your community driving. One of your cars was getting a little old and beginning to need a few repairs.

Since you still had another 16 months of payments to make on the car, you both reasoned you may as well make those payments on a newer vehicle that was less likely to need any repairs. Plus you rationalized the extra room would be more convenient for getting the kids back and forth to their soccer and baseball games and running various errands.

You didn't see any reason a car payment that was $50 to $75 more per month would be any problem because you'd gotten a raise, so when the payment on the great looking, late model SUV you found and fell in love with was $110 more than your current one you were a little wary, but you knew another $35 more than you planned on paying for the vehicle you really wanted wouldn't break you. Plus, the one you found was a great deal at the price you talked the salesman into going down to.

It was more luxurious than you ever thought you'd be able to afford, was made by a prestigious car maker, and honestly; it looked damn good pulling in and out of your garage and made you feel proud to be driving it! The salesman was even able to work an extended warranty in for your peace of mind for just $10 of that extra $35 per month.

True, you did run up a little more credit card debt than you planned, but no more than any other average family based on your conversations with your friends, family, and coworkers.

There would always be unforeseen things that had to be bought for your growing kids like clothes, sports equipment, and school supplies, *(and of course you always spent a little more than you planned on while having a good time on vacations)* but again, no more than anyone else as far as you could see.

All told, the total of the minimum monthly payments on all your credit cards came to less than $97, which was only about $56 more than they were when you moved in the house.

Could you be faulted for the unexpected new expenses in your life? You don't see how. You had no way of knowing that within a year your oldest daughter would need braces, which added a $110 monthly expense for the next three years.

And what could you do about the fact that when your company moved your offices to a new location downtown you had to begin paying for parking? That was $55 bucks extra per month you hadn't counted on but it was something you just had to deal with. You sure as hell gotta work right?

Was it your fault your idiot city government raised your property taxes by $60 per month to pay for a new $720 million stadium, all for a football team that hadn't won more than 6 games in a season since Karl Rove first took office as President? *(Oops, I mean Donald Rumsfeld. No wait... George Bush. Yeah, George Bush.)*

Now it's true, if you could have predicted all that then maybe you wouldn't have decided to get your pool table and exercise equipment for the basement at $54 per month financing, but for only $54 bucks, maybe not.

What's so puzzling to you though is that before you made each of these purchases, you and your spouse talked through the figures to make sure you could afford the payment, and each time you agreed it shouldn't be a problem. You even picked up a few hours a week at a second job to make sure you could cover all your expenses.

You sure as heck weren't rich, and finances were a little tight now and then, *but no more than anyone else.* Everything was humming along fine, and your family was happy.

Then your spouse's position at work was eliminated and they had to move to a job in a new department making just under $5 less per hour, *and everything went to hell.* Quickly.

I Don't Get It...

Which is what perplexes you most of all, because when this happened, following the advice of a financial advisor who attends your church, you both made what seemed a very smart move. You refinanced your home and paid off _all_ of the outstanding debt you'd racked up.

This meant now you only had one check to write, by one due date each month, and even though your new mortgage payment was higher than before, it came out $560 lower per month than all the bills you were paying before the refinance! How could that have not solved the problem?

"What the #*&@% happened?!" You curse at yourself in your head angrily. *"How did I get myself into this mess?!"*

You're yanked back out of your bewildered and frustrated thoughts without an answer by the tug of your youngest child pulling on your jacket. The child's face reflects pure terror as they whimper, *"Where are we going to live now? Are we going to have to live on the street like the people on TV? Will we be safe? What's going to happen to us now?!"*

You blink back tears.

Attempting a smile, you're weakly fumbling for an answer to comfort your child, but no words will come.

You have no answer to give.

You have watched your family's wonderful life come crashing down around you in what seems like just the past 90 days and you still truly have no idea what happened... or what will happen to all of you over the next 30 days.

"What am I going to do? How are we going to make it?" you ask out loud to no one in particular.

The cold, howling answer of the first real winds of winter is not comforting.

The Fatal Flaw

See, here's what's really wrong at the deep, dark, rotten core of this horror movie that thousands of well meaning, hard working people find themselves unexpectedly trapped in every day.

They thought they were on the right track, since they were doing what everybody else seemed to be doing, but they fell prey to the emotional disease we are all purposefully and systematically infected with from about age 3 on up, especially here in the good old U.S. of A. It's called…

…The Inability To Delay Gratification.

This is our fatal flaw friend.

This is spiritual cancer, and it leads to, among many other destructive and unproductive things, financial ruin and many a retirement spent stocking shelves at your local Wal-Mart.

My high school Economics teacher, Mr. Huckleberry, desperately warned my whole class about it every day back in 12th grade, though I imagine most of us were simply unable to resist the cacophony of persistent social pressures, celebrity voices and marketing propaganda coming at us from every angle, hypnotizing us into going the opposite direction.

Even though it was inescapably logical, -- *and I'm a logic junkie* -- I personally didn't heed his advice for most of my life, and I went bankrupt because of it, 170+ I.Q. and all. *(Hmmph. A lot of good that so-called "high I.Q." did me. They forgot to test my financial intelligence.)*

Yes, it's drummed into us from every direction. Instant gratification. Push-button results. Immediate satisfaction. Lose 20 pounds in 10 days. Find true love in 3 weeks or less.

We all want what we want and we want it *right friggin'* NOW, *(Remember Paulie?)* and most of us will do whatever we have to do, and pay whatever we have to pay in order to get it. If you're honest with yourself and consider your daily habits for a few moments, you know right now that you too are probably a slave to it.

Think about it. Go back and read the preceding sad *(but true)* story again.

All of those seemingly small and insignificant new expenses in the story came about mostly due to this "gratification sickness." And they all, bit by bit, added up to an average of ***$962 in extra expenses per month without even being noticed!***

That's an extra *$11,544* you'd have to shell out every year which, to put in perspective for you, is like the annual earnings of three illegal immigrants, and that's taking into account them being paid in tax-free cash under the table.

But wait, it gets uglier.

Even at the lowest tax rate, you'd need to generate at least an additional **$15,500** of yearly income just to cover those expenses. That means working 30 hours per week at an extra, part time job paying at least $10 hourly, and that's with no weeks off for vacation, rest, or the trip to the nearest stress center you'll undoubtedly need after putting in 70+ total hours every week with no breaks.

All because of the damned inability to delay gratification.

See, it kills most of us because when you're living under its spell, sometimes for quite a while, everything seems to be going okay. Then suddenly, out of nowhere, its effects rear their ugly heads and absolutely obliterate your life. Usually due, in one way or another, to a little known and insanely named phenomena I call…

The Curse Of "The Deadly 3-Point, 40 Day Amnesia, Ballpark and Idiot Fan, Exploding Fecal Rape Technique"

(Cue the old karate flicks music and sound effects.)

The touch of this curse is brutal. Here's a common example:

Remember how excited you were the day your beautiful new ultra-chic, home furnishings were delivered and you finally got to see them sitting in all their glory in your own living room?

Well, six months later you're no longer going back to the room solely to gaze at your furniture's splendor and smile proudly are you?

Hell, you're not even doing that just two months later.

Now it's just furniture. You're used to it.

Now you're grumbling when you're writing the check for the bill and feeling every penny of that $142.19 being snatched out of your paycheck every month. *That $142.19 that you really could use somewhere else.*

Not to mention you recently walked past a store window and saw a living room set on sale that you actually like a lot better than the one you've currently got another 2 ½ years of payments to make on.

Even worse, because of "The Vig," *(remember our old friend called "Interest?")* you're actually going to pay hundreds of dollars more than the original purchase price for the damn furniture you're already tired of.

Say hallo to my leel' frien', the first fatal dagger of "The Deadly 3-Point 40 Day Amnesia, Ballpark and Idiot Fan, Exploding Fecal Rape Technique:" *The 40 Day Amnesia Principle.*

Why The Hell Did I Buy This?!

The 40 Day Amnesia Principle states that no matter how much you fall in love with almost anything you want to purchase, no matter how much as Spike Lee might say, "you just gotta have it," within 40 days after buying it you will forget what it was that made you want the thing so badly in the first place. You'll often even find yourself interrogating loved ones, demanding that they remind you of just why the hell you couldn't live without it, since you are now so unexcited about it.

Just think honestly about the last five purchases you've made. You'll find yourself shaking your head and smiling about the indisputable truth of this one. It applies to all manner of stuff, both large and small, including shoes, clothes, cars, homes, and -- *from what many married people confide in me privately* -- even spouses. Of course, the bigger the purchase, the more truly fucking brutal it is.

The next component of this deadly curse is what I call: ***The Ballpark Error.*** Here's how it works...

As you sat deciding whether or not to buy and take on the $142.19 monthly payment for the new furniture you just had to have, you figured your expenses in your head something like this;

*"Let's see, together we bring home about $4,300 per month **(ballpark figure)**. Our mortgage is about $1,100 **(ballpark figure)**, our car payments are about $360 and $275 so that's about $700 together **(ballpark figure)**, then the insurance is about a couple hundred **(ballpark figure)**. Our gas bill is about $150 **(definite ballpark)**, electric's about $60 **(ballpark)**, home phone is maybe $50 **(ballpark)**, for the cellphones, including the kids, we pay like $120 on the family plan for all four together **(delusional ballpark)**. I'd say maybe $200 **(ballpark)** a month on the credit cards."*

*"So if we add all those up and deduct 'em from our take home pay, we've got like, $1,700 bucks **(ballpark)** left, so we oughta be able to handle another $142.00 bucks **(ballpark)** pretty easily!"*

You're a little surprised yourself at how much cash your household apparently has left over every month! It certainly doesn't feel like you could possibly have that much surplus loot, but since you rounded *up* when you figured all your expenses, you feel especially confident you're OK.

"We're good. Let's do this!" you proclaim, smiling confidently. *"Where do I sign?"*

Famous last words.

The High Cost Of Fuzzy Math

The Ballpark Error refers to how the "ballparking" of figures we do when dealing with our finances is often fatal all by itself.

It's the worst kind of fuzzy math, kind of like when the wealthiest country in the world says it can't afford to fund universal healthcare for all of its citizens but somehow is able to unexpectedly pull *one billion dollars per month* out of its ass to fund a war to forcibly "liberate" citizens of another country that just so happens to be oil rich.

Yeah, you rounded *up* on your expense estimates, but the big problem is all the stuff you left *out*. What about?...

1. food *($300)*,
2. clothing *($75)*,
3. car gas *($200+)*,
4. water bill *($25)*,
5. entertainment *(at least $160+)*,

6. kids' school/sports/whatever expenses *($75)*,

7. unexpected or unforeseeable repairs/maintenance/issues *(at least $100)*,

8. tithing/giving to charity *($430)*,

9. yard maintenance *($50)*,

10. Daycare *($400+)*,

11. Cable/Satellite *($100+)*,

12. Internet Access *($20+)*,

13. Security Alarm *($40)*, and most importantly for our discussion,

14. SAVINGS FOR CURRENT EMERGENCIES & INVESTMENTS FOR FUTURE RETIREMENT *($430 minimum)*?!

Total amount of expenses not accounted for = $2,405.00

Bottom Line: $1,700.00

- $2,405.00

= -$705.00!

As you can see, even if you don't have every one of the expenses on this list, not only are you _not_ going to have $1,700 bucks left over every month in this case, your ass is going to be in the negative!

Sound like an impossible scenario?

Well believe or not, a frightening amount of people at this very moment owe more in expenses than they earn every month and may not even know it, usually because on top of chronic "ballparking, " they are steadily playing with due dates, floating checks, paying bills with credit cards *(including other credit cards)*, and pulling off all other kinds of financial gymnastics to rob Peter to pay Paul.

Bad Magic

These are what I call **"Sleight of Cash"** tricks, and just like their first cousin "sleight of hand," the results they produce may seem magical but are illusions. This kind of magic can make you vanish and reappear in a bankruptcy court or a crowded homeless shelter.

The Wise Old Man With The Dollar

A kind, elderly man from my neighborhood planted the seeds of this wisdom *(of not "ballparking")* into my mind a long time ago during my early childhood.

Once when I was 8 years old an ice cream truck came through my neighborhood on a particularly hot, summer vacation day. Seeing my disappointment because I didn't have any money for a Dreamsicle Pop like the other kids, the old man handed me a dollar and said;

"Here you go buddy, now you can get some too!"

Yelling *"Thaaank youuuuu!"* behind me, I excitedly ran over to the brightly colored truck and ordered my favorite treat just before it pulled off. Eager to join my friends, whose eyes were already glazing over from an ice

113

cream high as they sat up in our treeborne "clubhouse," I grabbed the 95 cent popsicle, threw my dollar into the driver's hand, and ran towards them smiling and waving my frosty treat.

After we'd finished eating our ice cream cones and pops and licking our fingers, the ice cream wrappers, and any leaves we'd dripped ice cream on, we bounded down from the tree to continue playing.

The old man stepped in front of me abruptly.

"Son, that popsicle only cost 95 cents. You had 5 cents change comin' back to you. Why'd you run off without it?"

I'd considered I was due change when I gave the driver my money but, truth be told, I just was more concerned with getting over to join the crowd full of my buddies.

"Well, it was just a few pennies." I replied. *"You can't buy nuthin' good with 'em anyway."* I felt more confident in my reasoning as I heard myself voice this justification.

The old man's face hardened a bit with concern. It was almost, but not quite a frown. Then it softened again and he smiled at me.

"Little man, the pennies are what matter the most. You've got to pay attention to the pennies in life, not the dollars. That's what makes the difference."

As I stood looking completely baffled, he laughed and said *"Always remember that."* Then he sent me back off to play.

I don't know today for sure if that old man was wealthy or enjoyed a happy comfortable retirement, but later in life when I recounted this story to my father, he told me the old man had, at the time of our encounter, owned several apartment houses, 3 grocery stores, a cleaners business, and was the sponsor of one of my little league baseball teams. You make the call.

The moral to the story of course, is this: as the saying goes, "God is in the details." When it comes to life and death matters like your financial health and your retirement, you can not afford to deal in rough estimates off the top of your head. You must be precise and exacting. Every penny and every percentage point counts. Only poor people and those that retire broke think differently.

Don't think so? Ok, ever noticed how when you go through the drive-thru at McDonald's and order a Number 1 value meal that cost $5.74 including tax, they never say at the pay window "Oh, Just give us $5.70?" Hmmmm.

Now here's something else to think about. What if you pulled up to the window and the cashier said *"That'll be $6 bucks please?"* Would you pay it and drive off, or respond; *"Hey, wait a minute…that's not the right price!"* and insist on paying only the $5.74 flashing on the screen?

Exactly.

You might want to treat financial decisions that have the power to ruin your life and doom you to one day being an 'ex-retiree' with at least the same level of importance that you give a Big Mac purchase.

The Idiot's Song

The third assassin in the trio I refer to as: *__The Idiot Fan Effect.__* It can be particularly disastrous because it happens so quickly and easily.

You might remember the big story a while back about the Chicago Cubs fan who, seeing that a fly ball a player had just hit was a foul, stuck his baseball glove out to catch what he figured would be a simple souvenir.

However, as one of my uncles used to say, the poor guy "didn't calculate on miscalculating," and found out seconds later *(to the horror of tens of thousands of hostile fans surrounding him)* that the ball was just about to be caught by a player on the home team for an out before he unwittingly snatched it away from him.

This idiot fan's impulsive, poorly thought out interference had cost *his own team* an out in the eighth inning, and in the opinion of many die hard, angry Cub fans like my brother-in-law, ended up being a major factor in the team's eventual loss of the game. And the series. *And their chance at a World Series Championship.*

He left the ballpark that night under heavier security than President Obama touring small town Texas.

Let He Who Is Without Sin...

Truth is though, most of us often suffer from *The Idiot Fan Effect* when it comes to managing our money, and if we do so consistently, it makes a job-free retirement almost an impossibility.

We make long term financial decisions and commitments based on assumptions that could be wrong, and without planning for unforeseen complications that could occur in the future, and a great deal of the time we make them on a spur of the moment impulse. I mean, think about just a few of the egregious assumptions and omissions committed in the above story:

*Did you consider you might unexpectedly have to pay for $4,400.00 in braces for your kid when you decided to buy a house full of brand new furniture on 12 months no-interest financing?

*Did you take into account that you may have to replace a transmission 13 months later before you signed for a 60 month auto loan to buy your new, used car?

*Did you have a plan in place just in case your spouse lost their job down the road when you closed on your new home?

*Did you anticipate the housing market might slide into the worst crash in 30 years and leave you owing $35,000.00 more than your home is worth when you pulled the trigger on a mortgage refinance and used the cash to take a spare-no-expenses vacation to the Bahamas?

*Did you split 30% of your tax return refund between your retirement investments and your I.C.S. Emergency account this year, *as usual*, to keep the type of aforementioned unexpected issues from forcing you into bankruptcy or homelessness, or did you go straight from cashing the rapid refund check at the bank to a whirlwind shopping spree like all the other people who will retire and become Wal-Mart Greeters?

Chances are, the answer for you and just about everybody else would be "NO" to most, if not all of these questions, which is why most of our current financial situations are a disaster waiting to happen, and based on that fact, a comfortable, secure lifestyle after our working days are over is a deluded pipe dream.

Being repeatedly stung by the poison darts of any one of either *The 40 Day Amnesia Principle, The Ballpark Error*, or *The Idiot Fan Effect* can permanently damage your prospects for a job-free retirement.

Being hit by all three together… well that explains how the "Exploding Fecal Rape" portion of the curse got its name;

Basically… *it'll fuck your shit up.*

(Excuse my French, but hey, according to the Motion Picture Ratings Association as long as I don't exceed one F-bomb I'm still within a PG-13 rating, which means my 15 year old daughter can legally both read this book, _and_ watch irresponsible teenagers drink, smoke weed, and screw onscreen in a movie without my supervision. Given a choice, I'll opt for her reading this book. How about you?)

Look, no one can see into the future with 100% accuracy. We can't predict what and when unexpected crises and obstacles will pop into our paths in the future. What we do know is that shit happens and things change and we've got to prepare for this reality.

If you want to guarantee your ability to pay for your comfortable, happy retirement plan and avoid living miserably today, you've got to learn to think and plan ahead *before* you make purchases, you've got to prepare for financial emergencies in the future, and you *must* learn to delay the gratification of acquiring material things that have fleeting value.

The powerful magnetism of most of the stuff you're just dying to have right now is mostly due to the fact you don't have it. In almost every case, once you have the magic lamp, the excitement over the genie in it fades quickly.

Remember, 9 times out of 10, *just 40 days after a purchase* you'll be over the powerful allure of "newness," and if it obligates you financially for a significant period of time you might be very sorry you made that buying decision for a long time.

And when you retire broke and end up wiping off tables in your nineties, you will *definitely* be sorry.

So over-think financial decisions sometimes if you have to, occasionally miss out on a seemingly great deal if that's what it takes, but whatever you do, **Don't Make Long Term Decisions For Short Term Thrills.**

Your retirement depends on it.

Secret Don't #5 *Action Step*

What To Do Right Now:

A. From this day forward until you retire, commit to yourself that you will use what I call **"The 24 Hour Rule; "** wait 24 hours before you decide to go through with any major purchase or long term financial commitment, especially if it involves going into any kind of debt. This is what I call "The Wealthy Person Decision Period." It's what wealthy people do.

B. During the 24 hour *Wealthy Person Decision Period* answer the following questions:

* *Do I currently have at least a total of 3 months worth of my current living expenses in one or spread across several Security/Emergency account(s) that I can access within 15 days?*

* *Do I currently have at least 3 months worth of the monthly payments for this new debt in my security/emergency account?*

* *If I suddenly had an unexpected $300 monthly expense that was an absolute necessity, would I still be able to pay all of my expenses including this new debt?*

* If I had to save the monthly payments for this new item in my savings account for one year before I could get it, would I be willing to do so?

* One year from now would I still want to spend the total amount I'd saved up for this item or would I probably use it for something else?

* Can I purchase this item without making it more difficult in any way for me to invest my minimum amounts into my retirement accounts?

C. If you can answer "yes" to all of these questions, go ahead and make the purchase guilt-free and enjoy it to the fullest! If not, and the item isn't an absolute necessity, *don't buy it* until all your answers are "yes."

D. If you're *still* procrastinating, go right now over to **www.DontDieAtWalMart.com** and get your extremely valuable Free Bonus by signing up for my free daily **"Retire Rich Hot Sheet."**

Secret Don't #6:

DON'T
Bet It All
On Black

"Red 9 is the winner. Red 9."

The dealer at the roulette table calls out the winning number as she has all night; with no emotion whatsoever. You watch with excitement as a collective groan seems to come from every player around the table at once.

"Goddamit!" yells an older, gray haired gentleman standing next to you as his last chips are confiscated unceremoniously by the dealer.

A young, clearly drunk college kid, who's now down to his last $4 bucks, shrugs his shoulders at his fuming girlfriend, and across the table from you, a conservatively dressed, elderly lady in a red shawl *(who not long ago was repeatedly throwing up the "raise the roof" gesture as she won)* frowns sourly.

She's not the first person you've watched go from a joyous winner apparently blessed with beginner's luck; to a frustrated, veteran loser in less than 40 minutes. A few of them have hung around for quite a while, but you've been at this same table patiently watching every spin like a hawk for more than 13 ½ hours straight.

And yet you're still amazed that neither the no-longer-lucky lady nor any of the other idiots currently at the table seem to have realized what is so obvious to you: *the roulette ball has landed on 21 red numbers in a row.*

You've been observing this incredible run of reds for some time now with your life's savings in chips sitting impatiently in front of you, begging you to throw 'em in. You're finally ready to oblige them.

You traveled over 2,400 miles to Las Vegas for just this moment. The time is *now*.

Without the slightest hesitation, you casually move your entire $36,590 in chips out onto the roulette table as mouths drop open all around. Your cool, confident smile seems to unsettle even the dealer ever so slightly. The last few stragglers hurry to get their chips on the table.

The dealer speaks the familiar words. *"No more bets."*

You barely hear her voice. The bright lights and iconic 'ding, ding, dings' of the casino fade into silence. You're lost in a vivid mental movie, visualizing in detail the shocked and jubilant faces of the other players as they cheer in admiration for your big win.

The tiny, white, devilish ball is still bouncing wildly as the roulette wheel begins to slow its spin. ***"Time to shine,"*** you hear yourself think. *"Time to shine! We're almost there baby!"*

The wheel is moments from stopping completely and the ball is rolling towards a slot. You're not even looking. You're busy thinking about how quickly you can cash out your winnings, get packed, and get back home.

"Hope there are no delays at McCarran," you muse silently in the same matter of fact way you might wonder if there's milk left in the fridge at home and whether you should stop to buy some.

The wheel is motionless. The ball has settled on a slot. You glance up to verify your win.

Excruciating, Cruel Interlude...

Who would ever have imagined you'd hear those words spoken to you in your lifetime?

Your long drive home from the doctor's office unfolds in a daze and when you arrive you have absolutely no recollection of how you got there.

Turning off the car's engine, you find yourself frozen in the seat, too shocked to do anything but sit in your garage. The doctor's diagnosis of your soul mate's illness, the true love of your life, is still playing over and over again in your mind like a skipping CD.

124

"Unfortunately, without this transplant operation there is nothing more we can do to save their life. I'm sorry. I'm so sorry."

A $70,000.00 transplant operation is the only thing that can keep them here in this life with you, *and you're completely on your own.* The cold hearted machine that is your health insurance provider has made its final ruling. They will not cover it. They wished you luck with a smile.

You've tried everything to get the money including begging. No one you know *(and you've tried EVERYONE)* has it to loan to you, and no bank *will* loan it to you.

You've already sold virtually everything you own and withdrew your life savings but you are still short almost half the money. Short of taking hostages in the hospital like Denzel Washington in *"John Q."* *(which at this point, you've considered),* you don't know what else you can do, and a crushing sense of despair has enveloped your heart in your chest like a vise.

Then suddenly, the answer, the only realistic option left, hits you like a lightning bolt. It's so simple you almost brave a laugh, incredulous that it didn't occur to you sooner. All you have to do is go there, and watch, and wait for the right time, and it's a sure thing. You've done it before.

You start your car and gun the engine into drive like a bank robber, which is ironic, since you're speeding to the nearest branch of your bank to withdraw every single penny you've scraped together in your lifetime. From there you head straight to the airport without even a toothbrush. You ought to be able to be land in Vegas by 8:30pm, and be standing in front of a roulette table, waiting to collect the money to save your love's life no more than 35 minutes after you hit the ground.

"Don't worry baby," you whisper through tears, but with more resolve and determination in your voice than you've ever heard or felt. *"I'm not letting you go anywhere just yet. This'll work. It's foolproof. And it's got to."*

"It's just got to."

Back To The Big Bet...

Everyone at the roulette table stared at you like you were Paul McCartney marrying again without a pre-nup when you bet *all* your chips that the next number would be black, *but they don't get it.*

You happen to know that you've got just under a 50/50 chance from the start every time you put your money on either black or red, which are about the best odds you can get in Vegas, but *your* bet was a virtual lock because you figured the odds in advance.

It doesn't take a rocket scientist to figure that after falling on 20 straight numbers of the same color the odds are astronomical that the ball will land on the opposite color next. I mean, it's common sense if you just think about it. Hell, there are only 18 numbers of each color!

You watched this table for almost 14 hours without moving, waiting for 20 straight reds or blacks, and even sat through one more spin after the 20th red number just to be dead sure. When it came up red again, you did feel a sickening "what if..." chill run through your body, but then, you also truly *knew* you couldn't lose on the next spin.

Now to collect up your $73,180 in winnings, tip the dealer a hundred bucks for good luck, cash out, and immediately deposit the precious loot into a credit union branch right here in Vegas.

"I'm taking no chances carrying the cash home." You decide wisely. *"Not after we've come this far."*

You grab your cup of stale, watered down coke and prepare to leave, looking forward to watching the dealer sweep everyone else's chips into a big pile so she can double yours. Her mouth is moving.

"Red 34 is the winner. *Red 34.*"
"Place your bets."

You remember the room seeming to tilt and spiral suddenly upwards. Then the ceiling spinning wildly... Then blackness.

Through a thick fog of semi-consciousness, there's sudden awareness of cool air and a faint voice.

"Can you hear me? I'm a doctor. You've fainted. Are you Ok? Do you know where you are?"

Yes, yes, you hear; but you have no desire to answer. The feeling of grief enveloping you now as the grim reality of the unthinkable sets in makes you unsure if you ever want to speak to another person again.

Your only plan, the last hope you had everything riding on, failed; and with it, your last hope was extinguished.

All of your money is gone. Your days with your better half are numbered.

Sadly; You Too Are A Terrible Gambler

So, are you saying to yourself right now?:

"What a fucking IDIOT! Bet all your money and place all your hope to save your loved one's life all on one, solitary gamble with 50/50 odds in Vegas?!"

Well I agree one thousand percent, but what if I told you **I'm almost 98% sure you are making the same horrible bet on your life right now, *with even worse odds?***

Don't think so? Ok, answer this one qualifying question: *how many streams of income do you personally have coming into your bank account each month to protect yourself against unforeseen disaster?*

You starting to get it now?

See, yet another butt-ugly truth is that you are almost certainly, like our unfortunate protagonist from the preceding story, "betting it all on black" by wagering you and your family's lives, survival, and retirement on one, single source of income; *your ever-so-fragile J.O.B.*

And friend, if you've been paying any attention to what's been happening to the economy around the world lately you already understand that your true odds of getting and keeping any job until you retire, much less a *good* job, are *far less* than 50/50. Making matters worse is that if you *are* downsized, rightsized, or fired, there's no guarantee you won't be forced to take a pay cut at your next job when you're lucky enough to find one.

One poor lady from Indianapolis, Indiana I spoke with recently told me she was fired from her job of 14 years at one company and had to take a more than 52% pay cut at another company in the same field. Since she had no other streams of income to take up the slack, the resulting financial shock has her now preparing to file bankruptcy just 4 months later.

As my late father used to say, *"This world is not playing. It's deadly serious."* You've got to act accordingly.

End Of Days

By the way, it's time for another unpleasant dose of truth serum.

I know politicians and preachers have been promising you that if we can just get a grip on the illegal alien problem, the immoral corporations, and the greedy CEOs, we can bring back the good old days of safe, secure jobs until retirement with a gold watch and a fat pension, but it's imperative that you understand ***those days are gone and they're never, ever coming back.***

It's called globalization my friend, its effects are unavoidable, and it *ain't* going away.

We are now operating completely in a world economy. Every country's labor force and government is now competing hard for the jobs and tax revenue from the big corporations, and all corporations have a

129

legal obligation to their shareholders to pursue the greatest profits available.

Starting to get the picture? If these companies can increase profits by paying workers lower wages in another country, do you think some imagined sense of patriotism is going to keep them from doing so?

Sorry, but that's not reality.

Now throw in the shell games and downright counterfeiting of money going on in the financial and banking sector of America and around the world *(pick up Robert Kiyosaki's blistering book "The Conspiracy of The Rich" for a rundown of this criminal heist. There's a link over on the website at www.DontDieAtWalmart.com)* and you'll understand even more clearly how truly fragile your precious "job security" is. As a matter of fact, at this point, it's an out and out myth.

Believe me, I know this stuff isn't pleasant for you to hear. You may not like it, and your first inclination may be to flee into denial and reject this reality, but the facts are what they are and, to paraphrase Jack Welch, we have to deal with the world the way it is, not the way it should be. Get over it, adapt, and *prosper*.

Here's how:

How To Gamble (And Always Win) Like The House

So, what do you do about the fact jobs are about as stable and permanent as Madonna's next marriage. Go out and get an additional one?

Well, that's one option, and it can work, but there are two main problems with it:

Number one, the 2nd job will be just as, if not more, insecure as your current one, meaning you can lose it just as easily, and number two, there's no chance of a second job ever paying you without your having to work. *(If it doesn't now, that last statement will make sense soon.)*

If you do choose to use a 2nd or part-time job as an additional income stream or "plan b," make sure you follow a few guidelines:

First and foremost, chances are you get enough hard work and stress on your primary job to put you in ICU with a stroke, so for your 2nd job, pick something you enjoy or have an interest in so you can actually have your cake and eat it too. If you're going to give up extra hours of your life working you might as well have some fun *and* get paid.

If you love movies, try working part-time at a video store or movie theater. If you're a sports fanatic, look into a gig at a sports card shop, sports bar, or even at a pro sports stadium, etc. You get the picture. Think creatively.

Secondly, be sure you calculate the *net income* of the part time job to make sure the extra cash you bring home is actually worth it. Add up the cost of gas to drive to and from the job plus any other expenses, and deduct them from the amount you'll bring home after taxes.

Don't skip this step. You can end up completely wasting your time without even knowing it. I personally made this mistake once several years ago when I was delivering a major newspaper route in the early mornings. When I added up the cost of the gas to run the damn route, plus the resell value I was losing and possible future repairs I was creating because of all

131

the extra mileage I was putting on my car, I was actually *losing* friggin' money! *(only one f-bomb allowed remember... or have I already exceeded that?)*

Finally, have your part-time job's payroll department *direct deposit* the *first* 30% to 50% of your paycheck directly into your emergency account and retirement investment vehicle *(401k, index mutual fund, account for buying tax lien certificates, etc)*. If that isn't possible, then make the 30% to 50% deposit on each payday before you let any of the cash get in your hand. Then do whatever the hell you want with the rest of your part-time income. In other words, blow it on anything fun or enjoyable!

Did that last sentence surprise you? Well, that part is also critically important. Your mind will begin to associate the dual pleasures of watching your account balances grow *and* getting cash to spend freely, with the immediate deposits going into your retirement fund(s). In a matter of 30 to 45 days this powerful association will help lock the habit into your mind and your routines.

Whatever you do, do not, I repeat, **DO NOT** create new monthly expenses and pay them with the cash from this job. This is not its purpose. You need to be prepared for this job to evaporate or to get rid of it if necessary, at any moment, without any danger to your financial standing.

In any case, although a 2nd job can work, the best solution is to do what the wealthy do and have done for centuries.

Remember a couple chapters back when I told you if you were a late starter to pay close attention to the controversial guidance I was going to reveal to you in this chapter?

Well this is the point where I truly dive into it.

This is what you've really got to focus in on and jump all over.

This is the second leg of the two-legged strategy I personally used to create my own wealthy, happy retirement, and I strongly suggest you use it as well. So, here's what you need to do:

You Need To Create Another Stream Of Income By Starting Your Own Business.

And I want you to start it *from your home.*

"Aw Shit. This Is Where I Get Off..."

Ok, now usually in live trainings and seminars, this is the point where I get responses that include everything from blank stares to rolling eyes.

"What?! Why try to start a business?" they exclaim.

Answer: Because the biggest potential you have to earn 5, 10, or even 20 times more for your time than from a job exists in starting your own business, which comes in handy when your retirement plan is behind.

"Why start it from home?" they challenge.

Answer: Because just the tax benefits alone you'll get by running a business from your home can keep hundreds of extra dollars in your pocket and flowing into your retirement accounts every year.

Many are still hesitant because they think it takes a huge amount of money, time, and energy to plan a new business then get it up off the

133

ground and running. Good news. That's not necessarily true, *if* you choose the right kind of home based business to start.

Of course you know I'm gonna give you a sick cheat sheet for doing that. Pay close attention to the next section.

The Lazy Millionaire's Keys To Choosing *The Right* Home Business

Follow these "Lazy Millionaire" guidelines and you can't go wrong in choosing a profitable home based business to start fast. You'll find them especially valuable if this'll be your first business venture. Use the profits to give a turbo boost to both your retirement investments and yes, your current cash flow as well.

1. Look for a neglected problem you can solve: One of the best ways to ensure you have customers for your business is to solve a problem for others that is being overlooked. What pressing problem can you charge a fee to solve for people that they either can't or don't want to solve for themselves, and that no one else seems to be addressing?

2. Find the money in the couch cushion: The key word is *neglected* problem, and you know what problems often get neglected; the small ones? Look for profit opportunities that are often overlooked by larger companies because the revenues won't support massive payrolls and big operating expenses; but they're perfect for small operations, which is exactly what you want to run. I call this "getting the money from the couch cushion."

3. Make sure you either enjoy or at least don't mind performing the work: Look, it's great if you discover people in your neighborhood don't have time to drive their children to soccer practices and choir rehearsals daily and are willing to pay someone to do it, but if you hate kids, I'd recommend you _not_ open that business. Again, who needs more stress than you're already dealing with? For best results, pick something you'd almost do for free or at least don't mind doing.

4. Choose a low overhead, high profit margin service or product to build your business around: You may be able to fix computers at a $100 average profit per computer but if you have to buy $386 in parts for each one before you get paid, you are asking for cash flow headaches, especially when people don't pay or are unsatisfied with your results. What if your business grows very quickly and you don't have the upfront cash to order parts to complete all your orders and get paid? Can you say "out of business" and "possible lawsuits?"

Choose a business that allows you to risk very little cash upfront. Think "lemonade stand." Two bucks for 3 lemons and some sugar that can produce 20 cups of lemonade sold at 25 cents each, which equals $5.00. Subtract the $2 in costs and you end up with $3, *which is a 150% profit!* Repeat this formula over and over many times and you'll see how simple it can be to prosper quickly with the right home based business.

135

5. Choose a business that can operate mostly from a stationary or arbitrary location: If you have to do a lot of specific traveling to operate your business you're going to eat up a lot of time and money, which is exactly what can kill your actual profits. A good friend of mine closed his part-time lawn care business because he spent so much time and money going from location to location it didn't justify what he got paid for the actual work. Look for business ideas that can operate 90% to 95% from your home or from a low cost location of your choosing.

6. Avoid employees and inventory: I'm just going to keep it real with you on this one; the exponentially increased headaches, expenses, liability, possible lawsuits, paperwork, tax filings, and all kinds of other stuff that is as appealing as an evening spent with an encyclopedia salesman, make having a home business that requires employees and/or inventory extremely _not recommended_. There are plenty of businesses you can start without 'em. Unless you're the kind of masochistic weirdo who looks forward to trips to the dentist for tooth extractions, just take my advice and avoid them both like the plague.

7. Look for information age business opportunities: The holy grail of the home business today is one that taps into the information age paradigm. In a perfect world, this means a business that you can run from your home mainly via your computer, without inventory or employees, and reach out with into cyber space to serve customers around the world through the magic of the internet.

If you can discover a problem that needs to be solved and develop a business like this around it you will be the happiest camper of them all, and your retirement prospects can go from comfortable to flat out RICH; *fast.*

The crowning beauty of these is that the best of them can create income for you 24/7 and 365 days a year virtually on autopilot; even while you sleep. Sounds good doesn't it? *(Remember what I said a few paragraphs ago about you getting paid without having to work? Here we go.)* As you might imagine, it can take some doing to build from the ground up, but it's worth it.

I'm intimately familiar with these almost unfair advantages because this is the type of business I personally started out using to boost my own retirement fund on a part-time basis, *and it ended up eventually out earning and eliminating (thank you God!) my full time job.* I'll give you some invaluable tips on a possible shortcut to this potential goldmine in the next section, but just understand there are enormous benefits for you if you can discover, start, and successfully run one of these babies.

Again, it can be a lot of hard work, but I guarantee you won't regret it. One of the best books I've read that can take you step by step down the path to developing and starting one of these is called *"Internet Riches: The Simple Money-Making Secrets Of Online Millionaires"* by Scott Fox. And yep, I've put a link to this book over on the home page at **www.DontDieAtWalMart.com** under the **"Books & Tools For EZ Retirement"** tab. I also highly recommend snatching up a copy of Yanik Silver's excellent and easy to understand home training course called *"33 Days To Online Profits."* It can also be found on the website under the same tab.

Yes, It _Can_ Be Done

One fantastic and inventive example of following these principles to develop your own home business came from a lady I spoke with in Charlotte, North Carolina.

She lived in a neighborhood of very busy professionals, so she started an ironing business out of her home. The people would just drop their shirts, skirts, and pants through a small chute in her garage side door at their convenience and then pick them up the next day.

Don't laugh or condescend. She told me within 8 months she was making enough cash to replace and surpass the income from her former job and now she's able to be home with her children; _and she loves it._ Between the new income and the savings from no longer having to work outside her home she's now _tripled_ the amounts going into her retirement investment accounts. Sweet!

Now for the more ambitious... if you're bold enough to want to know the _easiest, fastest_ shortcut to a home based business that can be _wildly_ profitable, strap in and dive into the next paragraph. But remember, _I told you to strap in._

"_Aw, Shit..._" Part II: Here Comes The Moonies

Prepare yourself homey, because here comes the atom bomb; Without a doubt the fastest, easiest, most inexpensive, shortcut to having

138

one of these dream online businesses up and running for you, is to start a *home based Network Marketing/Direct Marketing business.* **The right kind of Network Marketing business**.

There I said it.

Now you can relax the look of terror mixed with disgust frozen onto your face. I'm well aware you may think I've absolutely lost my freakin' mind now, but trust me, nothing could be further from the truth. But I forgive you. A lot of what you've absorbed from broke and ignorant people in society at large, and maybe even something you've personally experienced in the past has given you many reasons to think so. Still, remember the Mark Twain quote I shared with you earlier? It's "what we know that just ain't so" that kills us.

I know, I know, you've heard and read all kinds of stuff about 'em all being scams and pyramid schemes, and you know what, I can give you a definitive answer to those claims once and for all: *most of 'em are.*

And let's face it, if you've ever run into one of the usual network marketing zombies/fanatics running around going on and on about how they've joined the greatest business opportunity in the history of the world, and raving about their "upline's" $5 million mansion and $200,000 car with that strange, insane gleam in their widened eyes, like I said; you have good reason to be afraid. *They are downright fuckin' scary.*

I call 'em "MLM Moonies" but actually, they're much worse. The Moonies usually ask you politely for a donation, and only *once.*

These nuts will pester you more than a horny high school boy at the prom, and will even trick you over to their house, or to a hotel conference room, or onto a phone call with their "mentor and expert in the company,"

139

then they ambush you with their upline "business partner," *(who usually hasn't had an ounce of success in the business themselves, by the way)* who then proceeds to try to strong arm sell you into their business opportunity as forcefully as the best time-share salesman alive.

As I said, the key is to start *the right kind* of network marketing business. If you come across anybody trying to get you to do any of the stuff I just talked about, run like you're Sarah Palin and you just woke up in a Mosque. None of that "Old Paradigm" stuff works effectively in today's environment, and most importantly, it's unpleasant as hell to do.

So let's talk about what you *should* be looking for in a network marketing/direct marketing business so if you do choose this route, you don't waste your time, energy, and hard earned money. But first, considering all the crazy, negative stuff you've surely heard and what I've confirmed, why even getting involved in the first place? Read on carefully.

If You Don't Read These Next Few Paragraphs, You're Going To Lose <u>BIG</u> In A Network Marketing Home Biz

The beauty of a network marketing *(NM)* or direct marketing home business as compared to starting your own information age business from scratch is you don't have to spend the considerable time and money discovering a business niche, developing a business plan, refining a product, and then building a business operating system from the ground up.

With an ideal network marketing vehicle all of that is done for you, so your start up costs in time and loot compared to the traditional alternative are a joke.

You can usually get everything you need to get started immediately in your own home networking business for $500 bucks or less, with a maximum of normally no more than $2,500 to gain entry into one of the more elite "Top Tier" home businesses, which generally produce higher profit margins and considerably larger cash flows.

Another huge advantage of the network marketing business model that cannot be overemphasized is your ability to leverage other people's efforts while compensating them in training, mentoring, and support instead *of money from your pocket.* Earning small percentages of the income generated by people who join your business organization can lead to some serious checks being deposited into your bank account over time, and with a networking home business; *(and you really need to be clear on this) the main goal is to grow an asset over time that can provide an increasing stream of income for you over the next 10, 20, or 30 years,* or even for the rest of your life.

Before you even consider getting involved however, there are two distinct categories you need to be aware of, and which one is the best fit for you is going to depend on your personal goals, your level of commitment, and your resources. Not understanding or being aware of these different "tiers" is one of the biggest mistakes people make coming into the networking industry, and can lead to some *real ugly* horror stories and expensive failures.

Tier 1: The Entry Tier N.M. Business

About 95% to 98% of all network marketing businesses fall into this category but the name can be a bit misleading. This tier is called "Entry" not because it is only for entry level and beginners *(there are plenty of vets still playing here and making some big money, to the tune of multiple 6 and 7 figures)*, but because it is where *most* people enter the network marketing industry, and that's because it is easier to get into.

Generally the cost of getting started in an Entry Tier networking business is about $500, but I've seen them as low as $50. *Anybody* who really wants to start a home business can get into one of these so this could be a great fit for you if you're really short on money. However, this is also both the blessing and the curse of this tier.

The low cost and ease of entry attracts a lot of hobbyists, curious people willing to *"give it a try"* but not seriously committed, the *"on fire today, discouraged tomorrow"* types, shady characters looking to prey on the weak, and *"get rich quick junkies"* looking for the next, big thing. These are the types of people who often come into this tier quickly, but also disappear quickly, so be aware. Most of them will be H.M. *(high maintenance.)*

And herein lies the rub because since your commission on the products being sold in Entry Tier businesses is often a very small percentage, you'll usually either need to sell a lot of product to turn a profit, or you'll have to recruit a very large group of other people into your marketing organization as distributors in order to profit off of override commissions on their sales. This can lead to big money, but it takes time and patience, *because most of them will be from that same H.M. group.*

Also, in some of these businesses, the only realistic market for the product you're marketing is people who are buying it because they want to join the business opportunity to make money. In this case, know that without a strong base of "product customers," you'll have to recruit distributors nonstop to make money. I'm just sayin... choose the product you're marketing carefully.

This tier is an especially good fit if you're primarily looking to supplement the income from your job with an extra $300 to $1000 per month, and if you have the determination, drive, and persistence, you can experience major success in an Entry Tier network marketing business, just know going in that it will take longer for the large commissions to start flowing in and one of the biggest keys for success will be for you to develop strong people, communication, and leadership skills. Not willing to do this? Pass on it.

Tier 2: The Top Tier N.M. Business

Top tier network marketing or direct marketing ventures are more popular with more ambitious entrepreneurs, experienced networkers, and veteran business owners tired of the long hours, prohibitive expenses, and financial risk of traditional businesses, and looking to create bigger incomes more quickly. They want the increased freedom of working fewer hours, from home, and on their own schedule. Hell, if you're a traditional business owner wrestling with the headaches of payrolls, soaring costs of doing business, dwindling customer bases, and evaporating profit margins who just read that, you're most likely thinking right now; *"Shit, what's not to like?!!"*

I hear ya. That's exactly what I said.

And if you're that same business owner fighting all those expensive, exhausting battles most employees don't even know exist, you can certainly testify that it's true when I say that if $2,500 bucks to start your own business doesn't sound like a joke to you it's probably because you've never owned your own business.

I know in my first traditional business venture I had to put a 2nd mortgage on my house for $18,000.00, then spend major cash on the operating expenses every month just to start a small recording studio that I unceremoniously closed a couple of years later having never earned a single dollar of profit. Well, many determined people *with no previous business experience* have started a Top Tier marketing home business with an investment of $2,500 to $15,000, spent $200 to $500 bucks a month to operate it, plugged into a 90% "turnkey" system, and built annual incomes of $250,000 and more within 12 to 18 months. Pretty easy to see the attraction right?

In contrast with the Entry Tier, Top Tier home businesses market more expensive products, but generally pay sizable percentages in commissions, often as high as %50 or more. It's not uncommon to earn a $1000 to $5000 commission and up on a single sale, which means, **and this is an important distinction;** *you can usually build a serious 5 or 6-figure income in this type of business based on your own efforts.* That said, these

144

products often have a hungry and willing, but very specific target market and learning to reach and sell the products to that market is *the catch*. Making sure there is a strong training system in place to teach you exactly how to do this is maybe THE most important consideration before you start one of these businesses. They are not for the weak, the lazy, or the hobbyist. You will have to learn real marketing skills to make one of these pay off... but damn, can they pay off!

As I said in the beginning, Top Tier home businesses attract more serious, committed, and experienced people, so if you do build an organization, the people will usually stay involved much longer and your override commissions will be larger. But the price of entry is higher, and usually so are the monthly operating costs, so your organization will be, in most cases, smaller than in an Entry Tier business.

Another concern is that people may have to apply and be accepted into a Top Tier business opportunity, so if you're looking to generate a large portion of income from building an organization, keep this in mind.

To succeed in the Top Tier, you DON'T need experience, and because you may not need to build, train, and motivate a large team of high maintenance distributors, mastery of people skills may not be as crucial, but you need to be serious, committed, persistent, and ready, willing, and able to invest the time and money to learn serious marketing and business skills. To be a good fit here, your goal should be to earn $5,000 to $20,000 per month minimum within a year or two. If you're looking to earn less than that, or you can't say with an emphatic "yes!" that the adjectives I used in the previous sentence describe you, don't waste your time and money in this tier. **You will fail.**

Here's the main thing: whichever of these tiers you think you might fit into, remember this; the key is understanding that *network marketing is not a magic slot machine.* Even though you can achieve massive success and some stunning incomes working a few hours per week, **it <u>will</u> take real work and effort to achieve results.** Anyone that says different is a crook. *RUN from them.*

But tiers aside, just in case I haven't beat this point hard enough, I'll repeat it again; *it's critically important to avoid getting mixed up in the wrong network marketing business.* Take it from someone who, before finding success; wasted a boatload of cash, went through a ton of heartbreak, and lost a few friends to learn this lesson several times the hard way. You *do not* want to subject yourself to the slow, excruciating torture of joining the wrong one, so regardless of how big or small your income goals are, follow the guidelines below and you'll be able to avoid that searing journey through Hell:

The Lazy Millionaire's Keys To Choosing "*The Right*" Network Marketing Business

1. Choose a business that has a simple, 24-7, plug and play, online marketing system for selling your company's product and recruiting interested people *you don't know* into your organization.

2. Look for an online system that does the selling, explaining, marketing, enrolling, *and* training for you. The more of these, the better. Ideally, you should have to do virtually nothing but direct people to it.

3. Make sure you enroll or join with and/or have direct access to a person in the company who has had already had success in the business, and can teach you *exactly* how to achieve the level of income *you'd* like to reach. They must be able to teach you how to use information age marketing tools to find and direct people *you don't know* (are you starting to see a trend?) to your product and business opportunity.

4. Be sure the network marketing company sells a real product with a true market, meaning something people have a need for or even better, a desire for, and would buy even if there was no business opportunity attached to it. If it is a product or service that people are already buying this can be even better, as long as your product is competitively priced. If you are selling a health drink for $57.00 per bottle that has a clone available at Wal-Mart for $9.98 per bottle, you are out of sync with the basic laws of capitalism called supply and demand and you will *never* build a stable, long term customer base which means you will *never* build stable, long term income.

5. Look for businesses that have been operating at least 2 years and preferably 5 years or more. More than 81% of all network marketing companies go under in less than two years, and if this happens to one you've joined, all your hard work, time, and money invested will go up in smoke.

6. Make sure the ongoing system provided by your company or team generates enough "front end" or up front income to cover your monthly costs of building your business like advertising, training events, marketing tools, marketing system, etc., plus substantial back end income.

7. If a company promotes one on one selling and marketing to your family and friends as the *primary* way of building your business, *run* the other way. Do not look back or you will turn into Amway soap powder.

The Burning Question I Get All The Damn Time

Since it's no secret *(I've revealed it in many articles, interviews, seminars, and trainings around the world)* that the particular home business that eventually replaced the income from my job in less than 11 months was a network marketing business, the burning question I'm pelted with continuously is:

"So what network marketing business did <u>you</u> hit it big in, are you still in it, and how can I join it?!"

Let me say honestly, I understand why people always ask. Hell, I would too. anybody with common sense would figure;

"Hey this guy's <u>already</u> built a six figure home business after failing three times before. He's <u>already</u> done the due diligence on companies, tested a bunch of strategies and techniques, went through the mistakes and wasted time and money to find out what really works, and I'm sure there's probably hordes of people constantly clamoring to join his team, so why don't I just join up with him and have all those people joining after me end up in <u>my</u> organization, and making money for <u>me</u>?! Sounds like quick success and easy money!"

It only makes sense right?

Well here's the thing. All those points are true, but as for the details of my particular home networking venture and how to join...

I'm not going to tell you.

The reasons being; first off, my personal home business organization is <u>not</u> for everybody and I don't accept just anybody with a pulse and a few hundred bucks to spend.

Now don't get offended, I'm not saying you're *"just anybody,"* but it's specifically designed only for people who are serious about starting and running a 21st century, bleeding edge, internet based home marketing business that generates a *minimum* of $100,000 income annually into their pockets... *in the first 12 months.* This is not for hobbyists or people who want to "give a home business a try." It's for people who are no-bullshit entrepreneurs who want massive results. Yes, it takes a relatively small initial investment and just a few hours daily to run, but it requires real effort, persistence, and especially, *action* during those few hours. All of this is why you have to go through an application process and be accepted before you can join us.

Plus, keep in mind I now run several other different business ventures and I refuse to short change anyone who's serious and sharp enough to qualify, so a lot of the time I'm not personally accepting new members.

Secondly, my personality only makes me a good fit for working with certain types of people: self motivated, driven, self starters. I love teaching and helping people who are determined to help themselves, but I don't do well with handholding needy or high maintenance types. Hey, that's me. As the great Socrates said, "Know thyself." I know my strengths and handholding ain't one of 'em. There are other top earners in the industry that excel in that. God bless them.

But the biggest reason is because it's not the core purpose of this book. I didn't write it as a recruiting tool to lure you into my or anyone else's home business ventures or anything else. Trust me, my team and I have plenty of applicants coming from plenty of other sources.

This book is about teaching you how to fish for yourself in all your financial and retirement funding matters, so accordingly, before you consider getting involved with *any* home based business opportunity or even decide if you're right for network marketing, *before you do anything,* I want you to go over to the **www.DontDieAtWalmart.com** website and watch my special **"Home Biz VooDoo"** video expose' called *"The Six Figure VooDoo Crash Course."* It's free, and it'll give you a behind the

150

curtain look at all the insider information you'll need to successfully guide you along the path to making the right decision for *you*.

Since I released this video last year to keep people from getting scammed into network marketing opportunities that are bogus or bad fits for them personally, there have been so many downloads of it that it's crashed our servers a few times so it's clearly been helpful to a lot of people. Eventually I may have to start charging for access to it just to cover the costs of keeping it available so, like I said, go check it out now while it's still free.

The information in that one, single video series reveals some of the most closely kept secrets of the top earners in the network marketing industry, and letting 'em out didn't make me real popular with a lot of the big boys, but it will enable you to make an informed decision about how and where to really make money if you do decide to get involved. Again, whatever you do, don't join *ANY* home business until you've watched it.

After that, if you want to find out specifically about my personal home business venture I'm sure you can google me and find out everything you want to know and probably more. That's life in the age of the internet!

At any rate, now you've got a few choices for developing another source of income that will help secure your finances and retirement against the very good chance that your current job will go 'bye bye' much sooner than you hoped.

Whichever you choose, *choose something and do it.* Just be sure you don't have all your chips riding on your job remaining a source of a steady, stable paycheck, or your boss and the company you work for making sure your retirement is taken care of.

Don't bet it all on black friend.

If you do, you'll become another in a long line of suckers that painfully finds out why the house always wins.

Secret Don't #6 _Action Step_

What To Do Right Now:

A. Based on your own preferences and abilities, choose whether you want to use a 2nd job, start a traditional or information-age home based business, or leverage the advantages of _the right_ network marketing or direct marketing home business vehicle.

B. Before you consider getting involved with _any_ home based business opportunity or network marketing business, go over to the **www.DontDieAtWalmart.com** website now and watch my special video expose' called **_"The Six Figure VooDoo Crash Course."_**.

C. Make sure you follow the guidelines in this and all the preceding chapters for using the profits to further your mission to secure a comfortable retirement for yourself _before_ you run out and by a new Lexus convertible with your new income.

Secret Don't #7:

DON'T Bleed To Death From A Million Little Paper Cuts

OR:

(DON'T Go To War Without Bullet-Proof Armor)

"Please step out of the car and place your hands behind your back. You're under arrest."

The police officer's face is chiseled into the most serious look you've ever seen. He means business. His hand is on his gun in the holster he has just unsnapped. His partner stands silently next to him with a downright angry mask fixed on his face, holding a taser.

"Oh God, this can <u>not</u> be happening," your mind screams, frantically trying to wake up from what obviously must be a nightmare; but the cold, sharp pains from the handcuffs now cutting into your wrists make reality on this chilly Autumn day during rush hour crystal clear:

You are going to jail. And you don't even know why.

"Officer, this must be a mistake. What am I being arrested for?! I haven't done anything!" you plead, your mind still not completely able to accept what is happening.

"You're under arrest for grand theft auto, robbery, and assault with a deadly weapon."

"Wh- what?" you stammer, trying to turn to speak to the officer. *"No, no. No way. This is crazy! You've got the wrong person! Wait a minute, let m… Aaargh!"*

Agony explodes through your left jaw as the officer slams your face against the hood of the police car and you taste blood.

"If you continue to resist we WILL 'tase' you motherfucker!" he screams, now nearly at the top of his lungs, and less than 2 inches from your ear. You feel the fury in his hot breath blasting against your cheek.

"Now get your ass in this backseat without making any sudden moves or you know what happens! You've been warned!"

The ride to the county lockup is surreal. You barely remember it all in detail, but the memory of the disdained looks from bystanders *(including the shocked face of your co-worker and manager who just happened to be riding by)* is burned into your mind's eye forever. You are filled with embarrassment. Your wrists are burning now and your hands are completely numb. You can't even feel them.

As you're pulled violently from the back of the police car, you attempt again to convince the officer that he has the wrong person.

"Sir, there's clearly been a terrible mistake. I wouldn't dream of stealing a car or robbin' anybody, and… assault with a deadly… I mean, look officer, I've never even picked up a weapon! Please check again with your superior or something. You've got the wrong person!"

"Ya right. Of course we have! " He snaps back sarcastically.

"Let's see, the rented car and the gun used in the robbery were acquired in *your name*, with *your* drivers license used as ID, and the description given by the person you shot during the robbery fits *you*. Good luck with the 'it wasn't me' story asshole. Hope you've got a good lawyer."

Your heart sinks.

What the hell is happening? You feel flustered and completely overwhelmed, having no idea who to call or what to do to prove your innocence. You're still reeling over the officer's rundown of the apparent charges and evidence against you. How could this possibly be?

A thick fog is beginning to envelop your mind and you're becoming increasingly unable to think straight as you're led towards the small concrete holding cell, still shaken from being humiliatingly strip searched and finger printed after you arrived at the lockup.

A lump of pure terror forms in your throat as you look in at the jumbled mass of dangerous, scary faces staring back at you from inside the overcrowded cell. A few are grinning like crocodiles, and all seem to be waiting breathlessly to see what happens when you're pushed in with them. A fight? A robbery? Or worse… You're refusing to allow yourself to even consider what "worse" might be.

"Have fun *'Innocent!'*" the policeman sneers at you as he removes the cuffs.

You feel the his hand roughly pushing against your back and your body advancing into the stifling cell as if sleepwalking.

The inside of the cage is getting closer, but fear has taken the sensation of your legs moving.

Tears begin to well up in the corners of your eyes as you hear the heavy, 4 inch thick door slam and lock behind you. The chilling sound echoes in your mind, signaling possibly the end of your life as you've known it forever.

The Nightmare You Can't Wake Up From

As terrifying as this account is, it's even more so when you find out it's based on the true story of a woman from California, who was eventually found to be mistakenly arrested and innocent only after being locked up like an animal for months.

So how'd she end up in such a horrible predicament? She'd fallen prey to the fastest growing, most misunderstood, and drastically underestimated crime in the world; *identity theft.*

Described by many who've been victimized by it as "financial cancer," identity theft is 5 times deadlier than most people imagine because, as you see from the real life horror story above, it can devastate your life in a helluva lot more ways than just somebody getting a bogus credit card in your name and ordering a few porn videos.

Even scarier, if you don't shield and protect yourself and your family, while certainly one of the most devastating, ***it is only one of the many millions of little paper cuts that are lurking in the shadows in wait, ready to drain the money out of your life's nest egg like blood,*** and snatch away your hopes of a comfortable, happy retirement.

Fortunately or unfortunately, your key to a happy retirement with plenty of money doesn't just depend on how much money you can *earn* to invest for the future. I'll repeat, as I have many times before, the words of the classic book *"The Richest Man In Babylon;"*

"It's Not How Much Money You Make, It's How Much You Keep."

See, even if you follow all 6 of the other *Secret "DON'Ts"* perfectly, you still must not let yourself <u>bleed to death</u> from a bunch of tiny, financial "paper cuts."

The final step you must take is to armor your money in iron to prevent it from being killed by the mortal wounds of battle.

Your Mortal Enemies And The Maces They Swing

So, what are the biggest unexpected and often unrecognized "invisible" enemies of your plans for a blissful retirement, and how do you protect yourself from the tiny but deadly *"paper cuts"* they so love to inflict?

Well, here's a list of certainly not all, but of the most common, the most damaging, and often most underestimated culprits, and how to protect yourself from them:

*Paper Cut #1: **The Traffic Game -** *Fines, Fees, etc.*

This seemingly trivial enemy can be a real killer to your finances so let me say, first and foremost, *just drive the f@%$* speed limit at all times!*

Now spare me the whining.

Believe me, this was one of the hardest things for me to finally accept and obey as well, but I've had the cost of excessive or unpaid traffic tickets and the like ruin my finances in the past. I've also seen them almost destroy some people's *lives*.

Not that the $150 bucks or more that has to come out of your nest egg isn't enough, but the resulting points on your license from speeding and other moving violation tickets can also cost you more money every month on your car insurance, in some cases will now affect your credit rating, and can even jeopardize your ability to keep your job.

But what the folks down at your good ol' BMV and local government really love is when you forget to pay a ticket or miss your court date. Now you get hit for sometimes twice as much as the ticket in fines *and often more than that in court costs.*

Forget or decide not to pay this stuff? Well, then your license can be suspended and you may not even be aware of it. Now my friend, just get pulled over driving while your license is suspended. Whether you knew you were suspended or not, this means more points on your license and a possible arrest; and of course that means more money being chomped out of your ass for fees and fines, possibly the cost of an attorney which is *never* cheap, and likely missing of time and wages from work which could lead to even more money problems *(it could lead to some type of disciplinary action, including termination.)*

Got out-of-state speeding tickets you *blew off?*

Take my personal story as a cautionary tale; these can cause you unbelievable misery, financial and otherwise.

I few years ago, I went to renew my license and was not only denied doing so, but my license was confiscated on the spot. Seems I had 3 out-of-state tickets in Kentucky and North Carolina during my college days that were unpaid, and those damn things had gotten my license suspended in the state of North Carolina. It cost me over $1,164.58 to get it all taken care of and then I *still* had to wait a year to get my license restored.

Why? Well, I could have driven down to appear in North Carolina's traffic court and have the judge lift the suspension, but I was informed by the clerk there that if I did, as soon as I set foot inside the court office I would be arrested on site for some strange, arcane legal reason I couldn't understand. Is there a lawyer in the house? At any rate, suffice it to say, I waited it out.

Have too many total traffic issues? Oh goody. This too could get your license suspended for years or even revoked permanently. Then how will you get to and from work reliably? Whatever comes out of it, it will cause more hassles, which will inevitably cost you more of your cash, snatching it away from your retirement plan where it could be growing and multiplying.

Here's another stupid, little paper cut from The Traffic Game; did you know just simple unpaid parking tickets can add up to huge amounts in extra fees and fines and eventually get your car towed? Of course, this will always happen at the worse possible time and in the worse situation imaginable for you. When you go to get your impounded car back -- *after you pay all of your unpaid parking tickets and extra fees* -- the towing company holding your car will have its hand out for a big, fat wad of your dough as well.

161

Do you see the game being ran on you if you're foolish enough to get suckered into it? Can you hear the giant whooshing sound of your money being sucked out of your pockets, and your retirement plan being mortally wounded?

Without a doubt, the best way to protect yourself from the financial paper cuts of 'The Traffic Game' is to not get tickets, etc. in the first place, but if you do, no matter what, **take care of them the first time!** It will cost you 3 to 10 times more if you have to be forced to handle them later, which cripples your ability to prepare for a job free retirement.

Which reminds me, speaking of cars by the way, is the perfect segue into your next adversary;

Paper Cut #2: **Insure For Security** *(And I Don't Mean A Nutrition Drink)*

Ok, we all know by now that Hell is not really a lake of fire but eternity spent forced to listen to a succession of insurance salesmen, so don't roll your eyes and skip to the next section when I tell you this. I promise I'm not going to bore you into a drooling trance, but here's the truth:

You must protect your money and retirement stash from destruction by having the right kinds of and right amounts of insurance.

We just spoke about "The Traffic Game" and I know by now you're beginning to think correctly about your money, so I probably don't have to tell you how costly it will be if you don't have car insurance, but what others insurance is truly necessary? Again, as is always the case, the key is to make sure you have *the right* configurations of all your insurance.

Now setting up the right configuration, especially for your car insurance, isn't nearly as complex as your insurance agent or company wants you to think. You just need to get a few things correct.

First, no matter how long you've been with one agent or who they grew up with in your family, shop around at least once every two years for the best rates. If you find better ones at a reputable insurance company, ask your carrier to match or beat them. If they don't, *switch*; sending the savings directly into your retirement plan. Your personal relationship with your former agent will survive if it's real. You need every extra penny that can be saved going towards your financial comfort and security and I doubt your agent is going to kick any extra Benjamins into your retirement investments out of appreciation of your undying loyalty.

On your car(s), set all your deductibles to $1000. Trust me, statistically you'll only have *maybe* 3 accidents in your lifetime. It's a waste of money to pay more for a lower deductible you may only use every 15 years. By now, you know what to do with the resulting savings.

Ok... this one's controversial, so make up your own mind; but *it really makes no sense for you to pay for uninsured motorist coverage.* Why? Because this is covered under the collision or comprehensive portion of your auto insurance coverage! They should cover you for *any* collision, even a hit and run, whether the other party is insured or not. Check out the book *"Wealth Without Risk"* by Charles Givens for more specifics on how this works and why. It may be out of print so you might have to check the library or used book store. Oh, and if someone tries to convince you not to read it, *read it for yourself and make up your own mind.* It's your money. The man *owned* an insurance company for chrissakes. That gives him more than a little credibility, but didn't make him real popular with insurance agents and companies.

Also; **make sure you have short and long term disability insurance coverage** in case something unforeseen happens that stops you from being able to work for an extended period of time. Hopefully you can get this through your job, especially if it's your main source of income. If not, price it through several insurance companies. The last thing you want to do is have to drain your savings or retirement nest egg in an unfortunate situation like this because you're not insured against it.

If you have *any* kind of business, including a home business, get yourself personal liability insurance. You can usually get an "umbrella policy" very inexpensively and it can save your life if *(and when)* you're sued by someone *(trust me, in business it's inevitable. The smart move is to just be prepared when it happens so you don't get your personal assets wiped out.)*

Homeowners insurance is a no-brainer, but if you rent as opposed to owning your home, get renters insurance! Period. This stuff is cheap and it is crucial.

You cannot afford to unexpectedly have to use your money to replace everything in your home because of a tornado, hurricane, burglary, a fire that may not have even been your fault, or anything else.

And this is vitally important whether you rent or own your home; you must take a video camera and make a recording of both the outside of your home and *everything* on the inside as well. Make sure you show yourself in the video at least once and also, while you're filming, don't forget to read off the serial number on each piece of equipment in your home that has one. Don't keep the finished recording in your house. Put it in a safe deposit box, or if you must keep it in your home, at least in a sturdy fire safe.

If, God forbid, you should ever suffer any loss to your property for any reason and need proof of what was destroyed or lost for proper reimbursement, you will thank me and your lucky stars that you did this.

Next, both you *and* your spouse or significant other should carry **term life insurance** policies that pay out a lump sum just large enough to replace the deceased person's annual income when it is invested and earning 10% interest annually. This will help them continue not only their lives comfortably and securely through the rest of their working days, but also the retirement plan you were building together.

Example: if you earn $30,000 per year, your life insurance policy should be for right at about $300,000. Make sure your spouse or heirs know this is what it's for, not to splurge on that convertible sports car they always wanted *(at least not until retirement)*. You may want to make this a condition of your will *(which you absolutely need to have unless you want your loved ones possibly fighting off creditors and all other manner of sharks in probate court just to get maybe 1/3 of what you want to leave for them)* or, better yet, set up a trust to ensure it. Check with a knowledgeable attorney and C.P.A. on the best way to do this for your personal situation.

Again though, let me emphasize this should be *term life* insurance not "whole life," no matter how hard you agent tries to sell you on it. You can get a much better return by investing the extra money you'd pay for whole life insurance into your index fund set up for your retirement plan.

Paper Cut #3: Protect Your Identity... <u>*All*</u> *Of 'Em*

If the story at the beginning of this chapter doesn't create chills of fear running down your spine, just wait 'til *your* identity is stolen. You'll feel 'em then, only the chills will be razor blades.

Identity theft is epidemic and running wild around the world and put bluntly, it can flat out ruin you; financially and personally.

You need to protect your identity like it's your money and your future, because it is, *(as a matter of fact, it's more precious)* but what most people don't know, and end up paying dearly for, is that actually; <u>*you have 5 different identities that can be stolen and need to be protected:*</u>

1. Your Financial Identity - identity thieves can create fraudulent credit cards, mortgages, personal loans, investments, *and* tax transactions in your name that could cost you tens or hundreds of thousands of dollars in interest, penalties, and even prison time.

2. Your Medical Identity - identity thieves can steal and use your medical insurance info and leave you with medical bills for thousands of dollars while also altering your medical records in ways that could cost you your life. Imagine them changing your blood type info to their own in your medical records and later you receive the wrong type of blood in an emergency operation. Not good.

3. Your Drivers License Identity - identity thieves can steal your info and get a drivers license in your name, or insert their own name and photo under your license number, creating unpaid traffic tickets, damaged or stolen car rentals, points on your license, suspensions, and even crimes and warrants for your arrest *(remember the traffic game? Here's an even uglier, deadlier version you have to protect yourself from).* This is how you end up as the main character in the terrifying story that started this chapter.

4. *Your Social Security Identity* - an identity thief can use your social security number to commit crimes or fraudulent transactions in your name, or even create a new, separate identity with a different name using your social security number. You could ultimately be held accountable for everything fraudulent or criminal done under your number without the foggiest idea anything was happening for months or even years!

5. *Your Criminal Identity* - identity thieves commit crimes using your identity leaving you to face the consequences, again, like in the butt-ugliness that begins this chapter.

I don't know about you, but I'm not real fond of the thought of some lazy, unethical asshole stealing the benefits of all my hard work and sacrifice building my good name; or of fighting Jethro and Jamar off my family jewels in a jail cell because some criminal sociopath created $100,000 worth of bank fraud using my social security number. Getting protection for all of these targeted areas of my identity became for me, no longer an option, but a must, and it must beome the same for you.

The only protection service I've personally found that covers all 5 vulnerable points is Kroll's **Identity Theft Shield**, offered through, believe it or not, the company Pre-Paid Legal Services, Inc. What's really sweet about this service is if your identity is stolen, they *actually work to restore it for you*, which is what most other Identity theft services don't do.

The others basically give you a set of instructions on where to start the brutally complex process of trying to repair your own identity, wish you good luck, then leave you own your own. It can be expensive as hell and time consuming, sometimes taking from 6 to 9 months to several years and thousands of dollars to restore your identity yourself. Some may relish that challenge of endless calls, letter writing, possible travel, and tedious follow up. No thanks. Not my idea of a good time.

You can get the Identity Theft Shield for less than $13 bucks a month *(no, you don't have to get Pre-Paid Legal's legal services to get it, though it is about $3 bucks cheaper if you combine them)* and I recommend you go check out the info on it, then sign yourself up and get protected right now A-S-A-F-P. There's a link to get all the details and even start your protection over on **DontDieAtWalMart.com.**

Still, you may also want to check out the info on another option I've placed a link over on the site to, called **"LifeLock."** It's a very good identity theft protection service for just $10 monthly, but it only protects your Social Security identity, which leaves your other 4 identities vulnerable. This is usually similar to what your bank, and credit card company, and everybody else these days, may be trying to sell you, but be wary. Some of those services have some major "gotchas" and holes in their coverage hidden in the fine print, and LifeLock was fined by the FTC recently, so Caveat Emptor.

LifeLock though, still is one of the original pioneers of identity protection, specializes in what they do, and according to what many people have told me, do it very well, which is why I also included 'em here as an option you may yet want to consider.

Many say it's a dependable service and it's definitely better than nothing, but personally, I figure the extra $2 bucks to protect _all_ of my identities and help restore them if they are stolen only makes sense, but you can decide for yourself what's best for you.

And since I get this question a lot; _YES_, thanks to our lovely identity thieving friends affectionately nicknamed "dumpster divers," getting a shredder to shred _all_ of your trash and documents with _any_ of your personal info on it before you throw it out _is **still** a must._

Just whatever you do, get one of these services, or _something._

I'd hate to be warning people with the tragic story of _your_ mistaken arrest, imprisonment, and bankruptcy in a future book because you put it off 'til it was too late.

Paper Cut #4: Don't Dump Your Cash
Into The Legal Abyss

It's sad to say, but in today's litigious society you can be sure of one thing: _soon or later, you will be sued by somebody for something._ And if you have any kind of wealth, savings, investments, property, kids college funds, or especially a business, including a home based business; you are walking through life with a big, red target painted all over your body like in those creepily cheery TV commercials.

They don't call it *"sUe. S.A."* for nothin', and as your wealth builds and you get closer to retirement, your risk skyrockets because you look like a bigger, better score to the ever multiplying leeches who want to take what you've worked so hard for.

Don't believe the danger's that great? All you have to do is go on the internet and google "lawsuit" or "is suing," and in less than 10 seconds more than 26.6 million results will pop onto your screen showing *everybody* suing *everybody* for *every damn thing*. And you know what? 10x that amount of people are looking at all these lawsuits at the same time you are and thinking: *"Hmmm. That looks like the way to go!"*

Good luck thinking it won't happen to you. Shit, "suing for money" is the new "screwing for money."

Besides that, there are endless retailers, hotels, landlords, property management companies, insurance companies, mortgage brokers, etc. who seem ready to screw you faster than Tiger Woods every chance they get. It damn near takes a letter from a lawyer just to get them to do what they're supposed to do anymore.

In both cases, it pays to protect your hard earned money, valuables, and future, *including your retirement funds,* by being certain the decisions you're making that could have legal ramifications and consequences on your life, are the best ones. Based on *the law*, not "common sense."

See, everytime you increase your net worth using the secrets in this book, you're also going to increase the amount you have to lose. *You need to build a relationship with an attorney you can trust for legal advice, guidance, protection, and to help enforce your rights.* Not doing so can be ruinously expensive to you with just a single onset of a legal problem.

You may not be able to afford to have a great one on retainer, but you must at least seek out a competent one to begin building a relationship with.

Still, lawyers aside, there are a few basic rules of thumb you *must* follow to protect your money and retirement investments from being unnecessarily dumped and burned in the raging furnace of the cutthroat, bottomless abyss that is our modern legal system:

1. - Don't sign *any* contracts without, at the very least, *fully reading every word,* and best case, having them reviewed by an attorney.

2. - Make sure if you start or currently run a business, that you consult a trusted attorney on what would be the best business entity for you to use, both for legal and personal asset protection purposes.

3. – Think long and hard before you join any board of directors and avoid this if at all possible. Individual board members can be personally liable for the actions of the board in ways that will surprise the hell out of you, and not in a good way. If you decide you must join one, here's another instance where I recommend a conversation with a trusted attorney first.

4. - **DO NOT** cosign for or put *anything* in *your* name for *anybody,* family, friends, or otherwise. Sorry, but the legal and financial risks *(among others)* are just too great for you. As a cosigner you will usually have to pay the full amount of the debt, plus all late fees and collection

costs if the other person goes into default, and statistically, ***more than 75% of all cosigned loans go into default at some point!*** That's 3 out of friggin' 4!

Those odds ain't too good are they? That's why I'm telling you *not* to ever play them. If you think your relationship with someone may suffer if you say no to their cosign request, what do you think will happen to it when you get stuck with 1/3 of your paycheck garnished every 2 weeks to pay for $22,000 of debt on a repossessed car that *you* never drove once?

If it's too hard for you to say *no* straight up, use The Blame Technique and tell 'em your lawyer won't let you.

Believe me, if you had asked your lawyer, it'd be true.

Again, follow the guidelines in these and similar everyday situations to protect yourself as best you can before you have to spend any cash consulting with a lawyer. *But...* anytime you're considering a course of action that could have serious legal consequences *(i.e.; you have something to lose)* and it's beyond your common sense, *consult with a qualified, trusted attorney.*

Now, if it sounds like all these possible interactions with a lawyer might be too expensive to be worthwhile, well that sometimes can be the case if you're not careful and thoughtful. But if you find and build a good relationship with a great one and you're prudent with your questions and requests when you do work with them, the time and money you'll save from being sucked out of your wallet by leeches will be well worth the small amounts you might have to spend with a lawyer on the front end.

Just remember this; a friend of mine who is an attorney always tells me:

"The reason so many attorneys stay in business is because people are always coming to us later, rather than sooner."

A clever alternative a sizable number of people and families in the U.S. and Canada are solving this problem with is what's called a "Life Events Family Legal Plan" from the company I mentioned earlier called Pre-Paid Legal Services, Inc.

After the legal mess I went through with my 10-year old, unpaid, speeding tickets from college, I've personally had this plan myself ever since because it lets you ask top rated attorneys unlimited questions on any matter you want, taking as much time as you'd like, get powerful letters written by them on your behalf when necessary, and in most states, gives you full legal representation on moving violations, *(this can save you a ton of time, money, and points on speeding tickets and has been worth 3 times the cost of the entire service by itself for me; told you I was a slow learner in The Traffic Game)* and almost 100 hours of actual legal defense at *no cost* if you're personally sued.

Plus they draw up a personalized will for you FOR FREE, and you get a "legal hotline" 800 number that lets you get an attorney on the phone at anytime, 24 hours per day, 7 days a week in case of an emergency *(would have come in handy for you in the earlier story, as well as for that poor lady in California, huh?).*

All of that for $16 to $26 bucks a month -- *which still amazes me a little* -- but the trick is, with more than 1.3 million members worldwide, the combined purchasing power allows them to attract some of the best attorney firms to do the members bidding, which is why they can charge

173

such a low price.

That said, one of the downsides is that often you may have to do some light legwork getting information to provide for the attorney working with you. Personally, I'm okay with taking 15 or 20 minutes of my own time to gather a phone number or address as opposed to paying an attorney $75 bucks just to have their paralegal do the same thing.

If you want to get all the details on any additional benefits included in the Pre-Paid Legal plans available in your state, as well as info on how to get its protection for yourself, again I've posted a link over on the **"Helpful Resources"** page at **www.DontDieAtWalmart.com.**

There are also a few other "legal insurance" plans available through some employers that can be alternatives to Pre-Paid Legal's Life Events Family Legal Plan and you may want to consider one of these if it's available to you, but be sure to get a clear understanding of how these work before you sign up for one. I had a bad experience because I didn't.

Many of them force you to find your own attorney that accepts payments from their plan, and you often have to pay out of your own pocket first and then be reimbursed. This can be tough when a legal crisis pops up unexpectedly, as they usually do.

Like I said, I had a less than desirable experience with one of these plans a few years ago. A serious legal issue came up where I needed help right away and I found it difficult, under those pressing circumstances, to find a good lawyer to represent me who would accept my employer's legal insurance plan. I finally just had to basically settle for the first one that would take me, and their performance left more than a little to be desired. I still have some unresolved legal issues from that incident. Not pleasant.

Not having to deal with these problems was a big reason why I signed up for Pre-Paid Legal's service later.

Also, a few lawyers I've spoken with since have said they shy away from many of these alternative "legal insurance" plans because of problems with long delays in payment and sometimes even refusals to make payments by the companies offering the plans. This doesn't mean they're all "bad," but it means as always, *you need to do your research.*

Choose whichever you feel works best for you; just make sure you use one or more of these strategies or services so you can be prepared and protected with legal firepower for when the inevitable crises do happen. Unlike in baseball, it only takes <u>one</u> legal "strike" to put all your hard work and financial retirement planning O-U-T.

Paper Cut #5: Don't Pay Big To Get Well, Don't Get Sick For Free

You know, when I tell you this you may groan, *"OK, this freakin' guy's just gettin' carried away now!"* but here's the real deal; medical expenses are one of the primary causes of bankruptcy and bad ass credit.

Your plan for a comfortable, secure retirement without financial worry can't afford for you to hook a siphon hose up to your bank account and let doctors, pharmacists, specialists, Eli Lilly, and the rest of "Big Pharma" suck all your cash out into their obscenely overflowing buckets.

So at the risk of sounding like your nagging mom, *you've got to take better care of yourself,* or put more specifically;

You've Got To Focus Your Time, Energy, And Money On *Staying Well*, <u>NOT</u> On Getting Cured Of Sickness.

It may surprise you that I'm discussing this in a book about **"The 7 Secret DON'Ts"** that guarantee you can finance your retirement, but you don't have to research long to discover the financial disasters that medical bills can create in your life. Surely you can see then why it's absolutely imperative that you do everything in your power to reduce, avoid, or eliminate them at every opportunity. The best way to do this is to proactively focus on investing your time, effort, and resources into creating wellness in your body and mind, not curing sickness. I assure you, *the "cures" always cost you a helluva lot more.*

Look, a lot of people enter the medical field for very noble reasons and I'm not saying all physicians are the enemy, but do you think your doctor *really* wants you to stay healthy? Before you answer, consider this question: do you think hookers want men to regularly have hot, nasty, off-the-hook sex with their wives?

Remember, all the money is made in drug manufacturing and "health care" by selling you all kinds and forms of "cures" for sickness, not in helping you stay well.

War on drugs? *Please.*

America is a big ass crack house full of drug *fiends.*

Just turn on your TV. Watch the commercials. There's more weight *(*meaning drugs – in case you are one of my particularly "un-urban" friends)* being slung on your TV screen than in south side Chicago. As we used to say in the hood, "Everyday, ALL day baby."

Ever noticed how once a doctor puts someone on that first medication for a "chronic" illness they never come off medication again? There's always side effects caused by the first medication, so then there's new meds prescribed to deal with those side effects, and then something else becomes an issue and there's more meds prescribed, and soon there's a surgery needed, and so on, and so on…

Add in the atrocious way most of us eat, the lack of exercise, and not getting enough sleep, then throw in ridiculous amounts of stress from our over-stimulated lifestyles, long working days, and multiple jobs, and it's no wonder most of us are trapped in an endless revolving door going in and out of hospitals and doctor's offices for treatments and prescriptions over and over again.

And even if you have health insurance friend, all this drains -- *often in drips and drops* -- too much cash out of your pockets that could be used to secure and fatten your happy retirement instead of your growing gut and the coffers of your HMO.

This goal of "staying well" is no doubt a huge topic and there's an overwhelming amount of confusing and often conflicting information and advice flying around out there. I recommend you start with a couple of books and resources I've found to be tremendously helpful, comprehensive, and simple, *(and most importantly they work)* then go from there.

The first is the excellent *"Ultra Metabolism"* by Dr. Mark Hyman and the other is Kevin Trudeau's eye opening *"More Natural Cures 'They' Don't Want You To Know About."* You can pick them up at most of your local bookstores or at Amazon. There's also links to both of 'em over on **www.DontDieAtWalMart.com** if you don't want to have to search

177

around. Also, grab anything you can find by Deanna Latson. She's unbelievable.

Now I'm not any type of doctor or health practitioner, so I can't even begin to act like I can give you any medical advice, but I haven't even had a full blown cold in more than four and a half years following these basic guidelines, so as a starting point, I highly recommend that you:

1. Begin to eat only organic, non-genetically modified food absolutely whenever possible.

2. Drastically limit eating out at restaurants and *avoid fast food altogether.*

3. Eliminate or at least severely reduce sugar from your diet, and avoid high fructose corn syrup and hydrogenated oils like the plague.

4. Gradually eliminate or at least severely reduce your intake of all over the counter medications, pain relievers, etc. Substitute organic, natural, and herbal medications as much as possible.

5. Get at least 7 hours of sleep every night and a brisk hour long walk *at least* three times a week.

6. Take 15 – 20 minutes *every day* to remove yourself from everything, clear your mind, focus on gratitude, and RELAX.

178

Get Your Free Gift Now at www.DontDieAtWalMart.com!

7. Make a conscious effort to expose yourself only to positive thoughts, words, and especially people, *as much as possible,* and avoid the opposite like your life depends on it. It does, by the way.

As you consider where to begin enhancing and maximizing your personal wellness, don't get caught up in "how much stuff you need to give up" or "how long you've been making mistakes," get yourself feeling overwhelmed, and end up just saying *"screw it."* Just start and continue gradually.

Make one change for 30 days and when you've built it into a habit, *then* add the next. Just take action to bolster your health and wellness NOW, and take it consistently and steadily. The results after just a few months will surprise you. After a year, you'll be blown away. I guarantee you'll be a completely new person, and you'll look and feel like one.

Combine these simple guidelines with the information in the two books I recommended and any others you find.

Not only will it make you wealthier and your nest egg bigger, but what the hell good is retirement anyway if you're only going to have 2 or 3 sickly years of it before you cash in all your chips for the final time?

Well, actually… *your chips stay behind.*

The Rest Of The Leeches...

By now I'm sure the point of this "DON'T" is crystal clear and I don't have to tell you again that there are hundreds of other greedy, money sucking leeches swimming all around you, just dying for their chance to suck your retirement cash right out of your tiny, open paper cuts.

Your task is simple: *starve the little parasite fuckers to death.*

As I said before, there are way too many to name 'em all, but I'm talking about the friends and family asking for loans, *(even though they chose to spend their own money on tons of shoes, or video games for the kids, or The NFL Season Pass on satellite)* the exorbitant interest and fees on payday loans, cash advances, and so-called "bad credit" credit cards, the mouth dropping mark up of rent-to-own companies, the ridiculous cost of cigarettes and habitual drinking, *(ever paid attention to how much money you spend at the bar or club over the weekend?)* wasted money on lottery tickets, excessive auto gas costs, late fees on monthly utility bills, etc, etc... It goes on and on. They're everywhere.

I'm sure you can add plenty more to the list yourself. The scary part is; if you add up all the money you waste in an average month on unnecessary crap like this -- *that could be going into your security savings and retirement investments* -- you may need therapy afterwards.

But look, I don't want you to stop having fun in life and I don't want you to live like an old miser huddled away in a broken down rocking chair with the heat on 58 degrees, wrapped in blankets and giggling insanely while clutching a jelly jar full of pennies. That's worse than being poor.

I want you to use your common sense, strengthen your self discipline, and make your first priority the building of your $1000 **"I.C.S. Emergency Fund"** *(that stands for "In Case Shit...," but if that* *offends your puritanical sensibilities, you can call it the "Security Accoount" ....you prude.)*

This will go a long way towards eliminating a lot of the situations that give these leeches an opportunity to do their thing. "The I.C.S. Fund" ensures you always have a way to pay for unforeseen necessities and surprise expenses that pop up without dipping into your retirement funds, but when it comes to making decisions on the frills and extras, *you've just gotta keep it real.* In other words:

* - If you have $37 left every payday after you pay all your expenses, don't buy a big ass SUV that gets 9 miles per gallon on the highway.

* - If you can't save up $300 to buy a budget flat screen TV at Wal-Mart, don't sign up to pay $52 bucks a week for 14 years to get one from "Madoff's Rent-To-Own." *(Yeah, I went there.)*

* - If you have to get on a budget payment plan because you can't pay the total balance on your home heating bills, sounds like you can live without the ability to watch every single game of the 2 - 13 Detroit Lions on the $250 NFL Season Pass.

You get the picture.

Avoid these financial paper cuts from the beginning or, if you're bleeding from them now, get 'em healed so when your extra money *(after you've paid your preset amounts into all your savings accounts, retirement investments, and living expenses)* starts to pile up you can spend it on living a fun, exciting life *guilt-free,* instead of handing it over to finance someone else's exciting lifestyle.

Living well now *and* knowing you're also guaranteed to have a fabulous, worry free retirement is the holy grail of The American Dream, and you can have it without having to apply a tourniquet and chop off an arm to get it.

If you just don't bleed to death from a million paper cuts first.

Secret Don't #7 *Action Step*

What To Do Right Now:

A. Using the examples in this chapter as well as your own, make a list of every possible "paper cut" you can think of that you've lost time or money to in the past 5 years, or that you are currently at risk for experiencing. Number each one on the list in order of priority, starting with the one that would be most damaging to your retirement nest egg.

B. Based on the recommendations in this chapter, decide what strategies and/or services you will use to heal or avoid these financial paper cuts and, according to most dangerous on your priority list, implement them in order as quickly as you can.

C. Make sure you follow the guidelines in all 7 chapters for investing any savings you realize into your plan for a wealthy, worry-free retirement for yourself.

D. Tell everyone you know who cannot *guarantee* they will have more than one million dollars in their accounts when they turn 65, to buy and read this book immediately.

E. Live a happy, healthy, wealthy, *abundant* life!

<u>Uncommon Epilogue</u>:

The Unusually Bullshit-Free Final Words From The Author

As I sit writing these final words to you, we're only a few days into a new decade and it's barely a year after the historic election of the first African-American president in U.S. history.

Being an African-American man who once sat on the verge of tears as his favorite teacher made offensive jokes about his African ancestors; in front of the entire social studies class, I can't tell you how much that achievement made my heart swell with pride.

Just as importantly, I like millions of others around the world, was enraptured with hope and the feeling that we were finally seeing another visionary, progressive, conciliatory, transformative leader take the reins to usher America out of the darkness of divisiveness; and into a bright, shining, better tomorrow.

And with the world economy currently mired in the most brutal, unprecedented recession in 50 years, we need all the damn help we can get, so having a president who's actually very smart is a good thing.

Still, at the same time… *I was filled with dread.*

I was filled with dread because I know that smart, charismatic, likable leaders like our new president often cause people to engage in a very dangerous delusion. Call it *"The Messiah Delusion"* if you will.

Too many people today like to believe that if they just trust the right person or persons to make decisions about their financial well-being, they can shift into auto-pilot, "zone out," and cruise control through the rest of their lives watching reality TV and reserving their most intense focus and brain power for fantasy football.

And while that delusion may be pleasant and comforting, the truth is still that as great, smart, principled, and well meaning a man as he is:

President Barack Obama cannot save you.

Nor can he, I, or anyone else for that matter, guarantee that you live a happy, healthy life free from money worries and with a comfortable, well funded retirement to look forward to. *Only you can.*

And you do it not through your thoughts, your words, your prayers, or your positive thinking, *(though all those things are essential)* but through your *actions*.

Simply put, what you choose to do, and often even more critically, *what you choose NOT to do.*

Open your eyes and look around at the lives people are living and what most people's retirements look like. Pop into a local Wal-Mart and study the look on the face of their obligatory senior citizen greeter at the front door. The truth cannot be argued; what most people are doing financially *does not work*. The road they are on leads to ruin.

But understand that you have a choice. You, like anyone else, can create a different result for your own life, but to do so you have to have the desire, determination, and discipline, to do some things differently than most do.

It will take some temporary sacrifices, and yes, you will have to disobey the new American Religion and delay gratifying some of your immediate impulses and wants. I could sugar coat that truth to make the picture more rosy, but it won't help you.

Yes, some people will wonder what the hell you're doing, and why you're not feverishly chasing a bigger house, nicer car, and the latest fashions like everyone else… *at first.*

Just know that their tune will change very quickly when they can't help but notice the ease, comfort, security, and joy you're enjoying in your life; when you no longer worry about money today *or* for tomorrow.

Take it from a former colossal, financial failure; who grew up sleeping in the same bed with his dad, mom, and little sister til he was 9, who hit absolute bottom by his early 30s, only to retire from his hated job forever just a few years later, and who now lives the life of his dreams with TOTAL TIME AND MONEY FREEDOM! I promise you. It will be worth it.

Please. Make your decision and take action *now*.

Don't procrastinate another day. *Don't* hope and pray for a fairy tale ending, and wait for God to drop a pot of gold from the sky enabling you to live happily ever after.

Don't accept a life of mediocrity and a retirement in working poverty like the greedy, rich, and powerful say is all you deserve.

Don't keep doing the same things and expect a different result.

Don't Die at Wal-Mart.